WHILE IN THE VALLEY

WHILE IN THE VALLEY
WALKING WTH GOD THROUGH DIVORCE

MARLENE JENKINS COOPER

Copyright © 2023 by Marlene Jenkins Cooper

This republished edition of *While In The Valley* is identical to the original work (2016), with the only distinction being a change in the subtitle and ISBN.

Publisher's Note: All rights reserved. No part of this publication may be reproduced, distributed, or transmitted in any form or by any means, without prior written permission from the publisher or author. The exception would be in the case of brief quotations embodied in the critical articles or reviews and pages where permission is specifically granted by the publisher or author.

Although every precaution has been taken to verify the accuracy of the information contained herein, the author and publisher assume no responsibility for any errors or omissions. No liability is assumed for damages that may result from the use of information contained within.

Unless otherwise noted, scripture quotations are from the Holy Bible, King James Version. Public Domain.

Scriptures taken from the Holy Bible, New International Version,® NIV®. Copyright © 2011 by Biblica Inc.™ Used by Permission of Zondervan. All Rights reserved worldwide www.zondervan.com. The "NIV" and "New International Version are trademarks registered in the United States Patent and Trademark Office by Biblica, Inc.™

While In The Valley/ Marlene Jenkins Cooper -- 1st ed.

Publisher: Songs of Judah Publishing, LLC

ISBN: 978-0-9961227-3-3

1. Spiritual Growth 2. Christian Living

First Edition

Printed in the United States of America

To my children, Joy Alison and Mark Anthony II,

I dedicate this book to the both of you. Thanks for being a comfort to me while I was in the valley. I am elated that both of you have accomplished your educational goals and continue to walk with Christ. I am so proud of my children!

Affectionately,

Mommy

CONTENTS

Foreword ix
Acknowledgments xi
Introduction xiii

Chapter 1 1
—— *Plugged Into the Source* —— *Jesus Christ*

Chapter 2 17
God Allowed It!

Chapter 3 27
Test, Trials, and Tribulations

Chapter 4 31
God Knows the Ending

Chapter 5 45
Walking and Living the Word

Chapter 6 57
It's in the Pen

Chapter 7 65
Give God Glory

Chapter 8 73
Fasting, Singing, and Prayer

Chapter 9 81
Jehovah Jireh: God Provides

Chapter 10 91
I Can Do All Things through Christ

About the Author 103
Feedback and Support 105
Also by 107

FOREWORD

Indeed count it a privilege and an honor that my friend and colleague in the Lord has asked me to write the foreword to her first publication *While In the Valley*. While reading this book, I find it to be a survival tool and learning experience on how to move on positively after being in the valley of despair, depression, and feeling hopeless as if this might be the beginning of the end of no return to love and trust again.

This is truly an inspiring book about how to cope with such a trauma as divorce when you start a marriage with excitement, togetherness, and a desire of wanting to grow together and mature in your love for one another as the years go on.

I believe that the death of a marriage can be a very traumatic experience, especially for those who have lost confidence in themselves, and confidence and trust in God. In spite of what has happened to them physically, mentally, emotionally, and spiritually, the God we know and love never forsakes us. This is especially so when we are in the valley of depression and hopelessness. He is an on-time God who will help us survive and move on in a positive manner. I say this with blessed assurance because I, too, at one point in my life lived in that valley of

FOREWORD

despair and hopelessness until God turned me around and made my brokenness whole again.

When Marlene gave me the manuscript to read, it was my story, that I was reading, and the story of thousands of others who have gone through similar experiences.

As a pastor, I am very grateful for her sharing her story of pain and then joy, as she came up out of the valley, and from that experience, she was able to turn a story of pain and sorrow into one of joy.

This is a book that I would recommend to all pastors to use in helping those who are going through or have been through such a traumatic experience and are now in the healing process. In addition, I would also recommend that the contents of this book would also be helpful to others who find themselves in the "valley" enduring other kinds of trials, tests, and tribulations in their life.

Thank you Marlene for sharing your story with the world. As others read it, I am sure that they will find themselves in your story, one of love and survival.

Your Friend in Christ,

Reverend Ethelyn R. Taylor
    Pastor, Oxford Presbyterian Church
    Philadelphia, Pennsylvania

ACKNOWLEDGMENTS

During the course of this arduous journey, God has taught me much about Him and myself. There are so many people I would like to thank for helping me walk through this season of my life.

I cannot forget to say blessings and thanks to all my sisters and brothers in Christ who prayed and encouraged me while I walked through this journey. Also, many thanks to all who read, edited, and offered suggestions while I prepared this manuscript.

To my deceased father, George Jenkins, who was the best daddy in the whole wide world, I love you. A real man will protect his family no matter what. My daddy loved his wife and children. He wanted to protect me from this difficult journey and tried to make everything better. Although controlling my challenges was out of his hands, he tried with all his might to support and comfort me, his oldest daughter. To my dear mother, Dorothy Jenkins, thanks for being the godly mother and wife that you have been throughout my entire life. I am blessed to have a wonderful mother like you. Thanks for all your prayers and support.

I cannot forget my sisters, Cheryl, Laverne, and Lynnel. Thanks for holding up your big sister during this difficult time. Lastly, to my only brother, George Jr., who helped me in ways that he only knows, thanks brother. May God bless you all!

Marlene Jenkins Cooper

INTRODUCTION

MY STORY

Everyone has a story. The story of this book took place during one of the lowest points of my life, while I was experiencing a separation and divorce. This is my story, from my perspective, as I experienced life in the valley. The valley wasn't always dark and dreary, but it was not always a very happy place to be. I am not the first person to experience both a separation and divorce from a spouse; however, my "valley experience" was tailored, personalized, and scripted just for me. I did not have the script to know how the experience would play out. Others went away from these same experiences with testimonies and stories of their own, but my story ended with God teaching me that "greater is he that is in you, than he that is in the world" (First John 4:4).

Have you ever heard the big "C" mentioned, and then a hush came over the room? The big "C" is for "cancer." When it comes to marriage, the next letter of the alphabet is the problem. There are only two ways to lose a spouse, and they both begin with "D." Those words are Death and Divorce. Besides hearing the "cancer" word that might be the cause of death, I believe the

INTRODUCTION

worst phrases one can hear from a husband or wife are, "I want a divorce," "I am leaving you," or "I don't love you anymore."

For nearly forty years, I lived the storybook life, with only a few bumps and bruises. As a child, I experienced living in a wonderful family, which included two parents and four great siblings. I was educated in excellent inner-city public schools, I attended one to two weeks of overnight Christian camping every summer, and I participated in numerous family activities. As a teenager, I enjoyed my Christian youth groups and graduated eighth in my high school class of 700. While in my twenties, I completed an undergraduate, debt-free degree in music education from The King's College in four years and obtained a Master's Degree in music education from Temple University. I married the love of my life, birthed two smart and wonderful children, and lived in a middle-class neighborhood. I maintained a healthy body, enjoyed great friends, and relished great educational experiences as a teacher in the School District of Philadelphia. This grand life continued into my thirties. Really, I have had few issues or problems. What a wonderful life!

Throughout my thirties, I was riding high on life and enjoying every bit of it! In my eyes, life could not get any better. Then, six months before my fortieth birthday, my nightmare began. Lying in bed next to my husband just hours before his fortieth birthday, he used the "D" word, quietly informing me he wanted to end our marriage. I said to myself, "Oh Lord have mercy! Here it comes! Here comes the BIG trial with life lessons to follow." Oh Lord, please not now!

Teachable moment number one was already in play: God does not wait for you to get ready or to get it together before we go through extreme life events, (i.e., death, health challenges, educational challenges, financial and relationship issues, etc.).

I was still in shock. I kept saying, "Dear God, no, no, no! Please don't end my storybook life. What about my children and all our plans? Dear God, no." But I slowly saw that God wasn't ending my storybook life. He was starting a different story from the one I had been expecting. I had thought I was in a fairytale that would end happily ever after, but I was coming to realize that my marriage would not have a fairytale ending. People's life choices affect others, and my husband's life choice to divorce me would affect my children and me.

The greatest hardship of going through my separation and divorce was experiencing life challenges that were foreign to me. Some of the unexpected life challenges were:

1. Marital status change – going from being a couple (married) to being single
2. Tax status change – from married to head of household
3. Loss of spouse/companion
4. Single parenting
5. Abandonment
6. Grieving like a death occurred
7. Preparation for a divorce with lawyers
8. Loss of income – from a two-income family to a one-income family
9. Loss of friends
10. Shock – realizing my storybook life was immediately changed

As I experienced the above life challenges, God began teaching me amazing lessons.

After my husband asked for a divorce, I placed my saved, sanctified Christian upbringing on hold for about a half hour. I jumped from the bed, cried, screamed, and swore loudly. Then I left our home, crying uncontrollably, and drove to a nearby Borders Bookstore, my favorite place to browse, read, and relax. I remained in the car while in the parking lot talking to God for quite some time before I went inside the bookstore. I sat in the

INTRODUCTION

car in the parking lot and engaged in a lengthy conversation with God before, eventually entering the bookstore. I believed that my cherished spot could bring solace to my spirit, with the expectation that the bookstore would provide a sanctuary. Unfortunately, it didn't turn out that way.

This was the starting point when God started teaching me about the real Marlene. I'd thought I'd known myself, but now God began teaching and making real to me great lessons of faith, dependence, and the power of His strength that I had only known abstractly before. First Samuel 2:4 states, "The bows of the mighty men are broken, and they that stumbled are girded with strength."

As I took time to reflect, my relationship with God was one of comfort. I'd even had the nerve to verbalize on many occasions that I was on a first name basis with God. He is my heavenly Father, right? I had also attentively listened to my friends when they rehashed the lessons God taught them as they went through their trials and tribulations. I always wanted to be a quick study, allowing their lessons to be my lessons, only without the pain of personal experience. Nevertheless, I knew in the back of my mind that God would eventually teach me humongous lessons complete with my own experiences.

The law of probability states that one has to eventually go through some type of horrific experience; I just didn't know when and what mine would be. I just never thought my marriage would be the center of my painful experience. When I was a child, and even as I grew into adulthood, it was difficult for me to identify with the people in my life who had lots of problems because I'd never really had any devastating life experiences. When my friends had problems, I often prayed with and for them, and was hopefully a support to them. But many of them said that I lived such a squeaky-clean, sheltered life that I didn't experience what others went through. Nevertheless, I prayed and went before the Lord for them (Proverbs 18:24).

INTRODUCTION

Well, how do you like me now? I have been through betrayal, separation, loneliness, sadness, divorce, brokenness, and a marital status change to single parenthood. Would the masses now state that I am more qualified to speak to the power of God? I am not sure, but I do have a story to tell. While walking in my valley experience, I have seen the power of God work in many of my life circumstances.

I hope you enjoy reading about how God made Himself real to me while walking through my most difficult life experience. My story does not end with a new husband sweeping me off of my feet and me starting a better, brand-new life. However, the story continues with God showing Himself as faithful, as His Word states. Isaiah 43:2 says, "When thou passest through the waters, I will be with thee; and through the rivers, they shall not overflow thee: when thou walkest through the fire, thou shalt not be burned; neither shall the flame kindle upon thee."

The lessons God taught me while in my valley aren't in any particular order. While I was going through my separation and divorce proceedings, The Lord gave me the title and ten chapter titles for this book, but I wasn't emotionally ready to write my story. Thanks be to God for helping me during the learning process. The blank pages of chapters are now filled, and I transcribed my story into words. Praise God that I didn't stop while walking through the heat of the trial, but came out with a story and message of promise and faithfulness.

CHAPTER 1

—— PLUGGED INTO THE SOURCE ——
JESUS CHRIST

*W*ho is your source? From where do you draw your strength to help you walk through the difficulties of life? Is your source of strength your friends, family, co-workers, or social-media followers? One can receive some strength and empowerment from the above sources, but where can we tap into everlasting strength? Life's experiences helped me discover that my power and strength came from Jesus. I plugged into the source - Jesus Christ. The severity of the present trial would test whether I would continue to rely on the strength of Jesus to walk me through. Could I really trust Him while in this particular valley? Was God's strength really inside of me and if so, would it be enough?

A very popular Bible character had God's strength inside of him. In the Old Testament of the Bible, Samson was one of God's men. The Philistines, a formidable enemy people group, wanted him dead because of his strength, but they had to discover its source. They paid Delilah, Samson's girlfriend, a visit and solicited her help to find out for them. Until now, Samson had kept the secret of his strength to himself, although he knew his strength came from the vow he had made to God, and his long hair represented that promise. However, Samson allowed Delilah to trick him, and after several fake answers, he freely relinquished the secret information.

"Cut my hair, and I will be like any other man."

Realizing Samson had told her all his heart this time, Delilah moved in for the kill. "Lay your head on my lap, Samson." Once she seductively lulled him to sleep in the false safety of her embrace, she relayed the information to the Philistines. As Samson slept, the Philistines cut his hair. Now they had a powerless Samson. They gouged his eyes out and put him in prison. The story does not stop there, however. His hair grew back as did his resolve to honor God. The story ends with Samson killing many of his enemies during a parade of the prisoners. Samson's strength was in, through, and because of his reliance upon God. (The entire story can be found in Judges 16.)

As with Samson, so it is with us. Strength is not a pill, a mantra, or a formula. Strength is a state of being, and it is needed while walking through difficult situations or problems. One needs strength from the beginning to the end, with all knowledge and power. There is only one person I know who can supply strength like that, and it's G-O-D. My strength lies in the power of God, in the Word of God, in the comfort of the Holy Spirit, and in constant prayer with God the Father. Second Samuel 22:33 states, "God is my strength and power: and he maketh my way perfect."

God is our source! He is our source of strength. God makes it possible for us to make it through our trials. We can victoriously walk through the fire because of leaning on God's strength. "Leaning on the Everlasting Arms," written by Elisha Hoffman and Anthony J. Showalter, is a hymn of the Christian faith. The lyrics speak about leaning on Jesus for strength and refuge. When my choirs and churches sing this song, it's done with gusto and excitement, as the singers reflect upon the strength Jesus gives.

Along with two other ladies, one of my past ministries was visiting, sharing, and leading a church service on Saturday evenings at a women's prison in Pennsylvania. One particular month, it was my pleasure to share a message with the prisoners entitled "Realize Your Source." I encouraged them to put their trust in Jesus and to rely daily on Him for everlasting strength. Whether incarcerated or free, God would uphold and keep them if they put their trust in Him. I was able to share this lesson with them because I learned and was reminded that God was my strength while I was in the valley.

I have learned and experienced that God's Word is true. First Peter 5:7 states that you should "cast all your cares on him, for he careth for you." God is omnipotent (all-powerful) and omnipresent (everywhere). Since God is omnipresent, while I am in Philadelphia, God is working out and helping me with my issues, but he's also helping my friend Darlene in Arizona, who lives in a different time zone and has a different set of problems. God is all-powerful, all knowing, and is everywhere. God has the time to help everyone who calls on His name. His strength and power are available to all for the asking.

The prophet Isaiah speaks to God's everlasting strength in Isaiah 26:4. "Trust ye in the Lord for ever: for in the Lord Jehovah is everlasting strength." However, God will move in His own time. God will work in our lives, but on His time schedule. His time schedule is often not concurrent with ours, therefore; we must wait, be patient, and know that God has it all under control!

When I was asked for a divorce, I resigned my position as choir director at my home church, but I continued as one of the choir directors at an area church in Philadelphia. I took advantage of the written prayer request time during Sunday morning services, which would be read and lifted in prayer during the Wednesday night prayer meeting service. Each Sunday, the deacons of the church asked for written prayer requests, but they never had to ask me for mine because I often had many of them. While at the piano and between musical selections, it became my habit to write two or three prayer requests on the supplied 3x5 cards. I knew God wanted to work on my behalf because His Word says so, and He also loves me. Upon the deacons' request, I loaded the prayer request stack with my prayer request cards. I knew who the source was and who held the power! The Word of God states, "For where two or more are gathered in my name, there am I in the midst" Matthew 18:20. I am grateful and thankful that Genesis Baptist Church consistently prayed for my family during that difficult time in our lives.

Yes, I needed God to work on my behalf. I had to daily tap into God's source. Praying and reading God's Word plugs us into the power source. Remember, Jesus died on the cross, was buried, rose on the third day, and canceled the sting of death. After doing all of that, taking care of you and me is a piece of cake for Him.

"Yield Not to Temptation," written by Horatio R. Palmer, is one of my favorite hymns of the church. The chorus states, "Ask the Savior to help you, comfort, strengthen, and keep you. He is willing to aid you. He will carry you through."

These words rang true in my life. As I walked in the valley of divorce, the words in Isaiah 26:3 spoke to me. "Thou wilt keep him in perfect peace, whose mind is stayed on thee: because he trusteth in thee." I truly learned that the Lord is my everlasting strength. I knew this in theory; however, the verse came alive during my valley experience. One does not have to go through a divorce to gain a greater understanding of God's Word; nonetheless, our personal experiences often open us up to looking at the Word of God and receiving it in a more personal manner.

It was during this time that I put the above scripture into song. In 1998, God gave me the melody and words for "Perfect Peace." Trusting and relying on God is all that I had. There was no other choice if I was to come out with my mind intact. Philippians 4:7 says, "And the peace of God, which passeth all understanding, shall keep your hearts and minds through Christ Jesus." I plugged into the source, the everlasting power source of God the Father. While meditating on Isaiah 26:3 in 1998, I wrote the following song:

"Perfect Peace"

Thou will keep him in perfect peace
Whose mind is stayed on Thee.
Thou will keep him in perfect peace
Whose mind is stayed on Thee.

Because he trusteth in Thee
Because He trusteth in Thee
Trust ye in the Lord forever.
Because he trusteth in Thee
Because he trusteth in Thee
For Jehovah is everlasting strength.

Only trust Him.
Only trust Him.
Only trust Him now.
He will lead you.
Guide and keep you
Only trust Him now.

© 1998 Marlene Jenkins Cooper

The worth of prayer was never in question to me, but the unknown end to my situation was a problem. The Lord taught me to confide in Him and gather my prayer partners as I walked through the divorce process. At the present time, I don't have an everyday prayer partner who prays with me on a consistent basis. However, I have a group of family and friends that I can call at any time. They pray for situations that concern me, and I pray for situations that concern them.

No matter what problems we are facing in our lives, God is here to strengthen each one of us. One of the first lessons that I was reminded of was that Jesus Christ is my source and that I need to tap into Him daily in order to stay connected to His power. Christ Jesus is the source in which there has never been an outage, a disconnection, or a malfunction.

Robert Ray's gospel song, "He Never Failed Me Yet," is a reminder of God's mighty power. During my valley experience, I felt that this song was written exclusively for me. It helped me to hear over and over again that God had never failed me. There were times during my divorce experience when I felt I had fallen into the depths of despair, and those few seconds made me feel more alone and vulnerable. Although I felt lonely, God often reminded me of all the things that He had done for me in the past. How easily we forget; how easily I forgot. God was there, He was in control, and I could trust Him. God has never failed me.

I am only human, and I know better than to think negatively because I have history with God. I have to keep remembering and recollecting what God has done for me years in the past, yesterday, and even on this very day. My choir sings a song entitled "Jesus, I'll Never Forget What You've Done for Me." When amnesia tries to set in, we must look back over our lives. We must not forget how God handled and fixed the trials, problems, and situations that have occurred in our lives.

Brokenness is a new word in my vocabulary. For the first forty years of my life, I never experienced brokenness, or what it felt like to be broken. During my first forty years of life, I had few major trials. I've learned something; just live long enough!

One famous television talk show host often asks the

following question, "What are the five defining moments of your life?" The ranking of the events can change based on other life experiences, and they need not be unhappy experiences. Do you know the five defining moments of your life?

My Top Five Defining Moment

1. Almost Drowned as a Child

When I was eight years old, I had a near-drowning experience in a lake during a one-week stay a a Christian summer camp. While leaving the lake, I grabbed onto the girl in front of me as she climbed out of the lake. No one really knew I was drowning. Since the girl in front of me was not aware that I was drowning, she became very upset that I was pulling and grabbing at her. I knew I was drowning and needed help, so I latched onto her to bring me to safety. Thank you, Jesus!

2. Violin Needed for Music Festival (1970)

While a student at Leeds Junior High School, I left my violin in my school locker on the night of a major student concert. The School District of Philadelphia's District Six Music Festival was being held at Philadelphia High School for Girls. As a string member of the orchestra, it was imperative that I had an instrument to play.

At 4:00 PM, I still had no violin. A violin needed to be in my hands by 6:00 PM. In 1970, there were no cell phones, emails, texts, or faxes, and social media hadn't been invented yet. My only recourse was to walk up and down my neighborhood in faith believing that someone had a violin I could borrow. I lived in a middle-class neighborhood where most children took group or private music lessons. God preordained it that one of my classmates would have her violin at home. Praise the Lord! She lived two blocks from my house. I could go to the concert, sit in my seat, and play my little heart out. At a young age (thirteen or fourteen), I learned God provides, even when we mess up. God is Jehovah Jireh – The Lord Provides.

As a youngster, I knew God performed miracles. Although the children in my neighborhood played many musical instruments, I needed a specific one – a violin! Who walks up and down the neighborhood looking for a violin? I did. Jehovah Jireh, the Lord provides.

3. The Announcement – January, 1997

Just hours before my husband's fortieth birthday, he stated he wanted a divorce. Brokenness was now immediately a part of my life. My heart was broken, my spirit was broken, and my family would be broken. Oh, how I hated the year 1997, but God taught me about brokenness.

The night of January 17, 1997, changed my life forever. I went from wholeness to brokenness in seconds. Humpty Dumpty, the character in the famous nursery rhyme, had a great fall, and all the king's horses and all of his men could not put Humpty Dumpty back together again. I now knew how Humpty Dumpty felt. But I was about to learn for myself that God can mend the broken-hearted and put the pieces back together again!

The pieces didn't come back together that night, but day-by-day, month-by-month, and year-by-year, with God's love, promises, and support, He put me back together again. I bless God that He has the power to mend the broken-hearted and the lives of people.

4. Marital Separation (1999)

On Tuesday, February 1, 1999, at around 5:00 AM, my husband, who had spoken of leaving the marriage for two years, physically left the home for good. I am not sure if this was the day that he had planned in his mind to physically leave. When people choose to leave you, they usually have a well-thought-out plan in their mind. The actual day may not be selected, but there is a plan. There may be several plans: Plan A, Plan B, or maybe even Plan C. There is a plan! Unfortunately, I didn't know my husband's actual plans.

Well, I got up, washed, dressed myself, and went to work, because life moves on. Nevertheless, I knew my life was going to drastically change. I don't have lots of words to describe how my heart felt. The only word that I can use is brokenness. My husband gave our children the news of his final departure from the home before they left for school. I cannot imagine how their hearts felt, either. How was their school day? Can you imagine learning concepts, principles, and important facts on the day your dad permanently leaves your home? Joy and Mark are not the first children in the world to have had to experience this, but they had God to help them during this difficult life experience. Brokenness is a terrible feeling and state of being. My children and I had to go to school and work and do the duties expected of us, even in our brokenness.

I'll never forget the day one of my middle school students took me aside after class after I scolded him for being late to school and to my opera class. He explained his life story to me. His dad had left their family and was taking care of another family with children who were not his. My student, his mother, and his brother were trying to fare the best way they could. Being late to school, and learning about Mozart's operas in my class, was not a major issue in his life. Since he was in control of his life, he told me it was his decision to attend school, late or on time. This event happened years before my brokenness. I cannot imagine my own children's teacher trying to talk to them about anything on that day – Tuesday, February 1, 1999 – the day their father left home.

5. My Beloved Father Passes Away (2007)

George Jenkins Jr., the devoted husband of fifty-two years to my mom, the best father in the world to his five children, a wonderful grandfather, a great son to his parents, a caring sibling, and most endearing deacon to the many members he served in the churches that he was a member of for the last sixty years, passed away to his eternal rest in heaven on September 4, 2007. It was easy to release my father because his body was tired, and he wanted to go home to heaven, but I miss him so. Nonetheless, my heart was broken again, but I had my daddy's love to heal it. My dad wholeheartedly served his God, family, and church. I knew my dad loved me, and he showed it my entire life. I miss his presence, voice, conversations, Biblical consultations, and love.

Although the five defining moments of my life were life-shattering, with the help of God, I could get through each of those moments. Some of my defining moments were solved in one day, and the other moments took years to be healed. The exercise of defining those moments of my life helped me to embrace my inner self, dig deep, and consciously decide on what events had shaped me. Through it all, God was with me.

God never fails, but I had so many questions and concerns. How would I support my family on one income? How would I cover the mortgage, heating, electricity, water, phones, cable, my graduate school bill, and my children's sports and activities? God didn't let me forget the words written in Second Peter 5:7 "Cast all your cares on Him, for He careth for you." Therefore, all people should pour the Word of God into their hearts. Isaiah 55:11 states, "So shall my word be that goeth forth out of my mouth: it shall not return unto me void, but it shall accomplish that which I please, and it shall prosper in the thing whereto I sent it." When we have God's word in our hearts, we can be assured that all that it says it will accomplish in us will actually happen.

Four days later on February 5, 1999, the roof of my home opened up in multiple spots during a mighty rainstorm, and water poured in profusely from every hole. Wait a minute! It wasn't even April yet! Wait a minute! Why couldn't the roof open up prior to February 1st when my husband was still in the home? This was my first challenge in doing things on my own with God's help. I prayed for God's help and retrieved some buckets. Collecting the water from the leaky roof was one thing, but how I was going to pay to fix the roof was another. Here was my first time to remember God had never failed me. Although I did not know how and I did not know when, I knew God was working it out for me. I stayed plugged into the power source, Jesus Christ.

The Lord provided the $1,100.00 to fix the leaky roof. I didn't have to borrow the money, ask anyone for it, or take out a loan. My six-to-eight-month emergency fund wasn't fully funded, but someone who knew of my plight sent me one thousand dollars to help me pay for the roof. Thanks be to God, who never leaves us or forsakes us.

Two weeks after my husband left the home, I lost my pocketbook at a teacher's conference at a major Philadelphia hotel. I said to myself, "Oh no! What am I going to do now?" My colleagues did not know that my husband had separated from me, but for some reason, nobody asked why I did not call my husband for help. Who would I call to bring me my spare set of keys? Would my parents want to come to Center City, Philadelphia to bring me my keys on a Friday evening? I used the hotel phone to call my various credit card companies and cancel my cards. I prayed for help from God and I did not fall apart. Later that evening, a Good Samaritan turned in my lost pocketbook with everything intact. (Teachers rock!) My pocketbook was given to one of the band members. We were listening to great music and having refreshments when it was announced that they found a pocketbook. Praise the Lord!

In Hebrews 13:6 we read, "He will never leave or forsake you." People will leave you, but Jesus will never leave or forsake you. There is nothing too big for God. God met every need! I knew God would never fail me, and He didn't. I choose to use every testimony as a testimony of God's unceasing power. By the way, everyone needs to have a six-to-eight-month emergency fund. I am still working on fully funding mine. An emergency fund is an account that houses savings of six to eight monthly expenses in case of a major emergency or loss of income.

Scriptures in the Bible give examples of how God came through for people in the past. Daniel, Shadrach, Meshach, and Abednego were in the fiery furnace. They were not burned, because you cannot touch God's people unless He gives permission. Daniel was in the lion's den. God shut the mouths of the lions and Daniel was able to walk out unscathed and uneaten. Esther went before the king with a request and her life was spared. My favorite God-in-help experience is the story of the Shunammite woman in the Old Testament whose son was sick and died. She placed her son on the prophet's bed and went to find Elisha. Then she went by donkey to find the man of God and tell him what was going on. Through the power of God, Elisha prayed, and her son was raised from the dead (Second Kings 4:8-37). In the New Testament, Paul and Silas were locked in jail and God was with them. The jailer and his entire household were saved while Paul and Silas were prison inmates (Acts 16:25-35).

Remember, our trials aren't about us. Our trials and tribulations are always about someone else. Someone else is reading or observing our story; we can give them hope that they can go through difficulties and come out on the other side. I know this for myself.

I could not believe Satan had the nerve to ask God if he could send me through my divorce experience. Satan didn't cause the circumstances. We all have free will. Choices are ours to make. Decisions are made and carried out. Moreover, I learned that the decisions we make affect the lives of others.

Remember, nothing can happen to a child of God unless God grants permission. God granting Satan permission was hurtful to me, but God knows His children and knows how much we can handle. The Lord will never put more on us than we can bear. A childhood memory of Sister Sadie singing Roberta Martin's song, "He Knows Just How Much You Can Bear" (1941) was music to my ears. The Word of God states in First Corinthians 10:13 "There hath no temptation taken you but such as is common to man: but God is faithful, who will not suffer you to be tempted above that you are able, but will with the temptation also make a way to escape, that ye may be able to bear it."

God has my back. When I heard the word divorce come from my husband's lips, I wasn't thinking of a great spiritual response. I have never verbally cursed anyone in my life before this experience. On this very day and at that moment, those curse words came to my lips and flowed freely. Lord have mercy on me! My response was the second worst carnal experience in my life!

My first most carnal cursing experience occurred when I was in the fourth grade. I had just been punished for poor behavior in school. (While in grade school, I never could control my talking.) While at home in a room by myself, and loaded with anger, I quietly cursed under my breath. I knew God heard me, but oops, my mom heard me too. (My middle school students always told me I could never whisper quietly! I should have learned this when I was a child.) The extreme punishment I received from my mother for cursing as a child cured me for life until I was asked for a divorce. I had a one-day relapse. Thanks be to God because He forgives! (First John 1:9).

I have taken His promises and held them dear to my heart.

God has never failed me. I had to gather all the scriptures I knew, hold on to them for dear life, and remain plugged into the Source, Jesus Christ. During the divorce process, I read and sang the scriptures and listened to others speak on the scriptures from God's Holy Word, all of which helped me to stay plugged into the power source, Jesus Christ. He has never failed me. I have failed Him multiple times, but He has never failed me. I have history with God, and I have great testimonies of what He has done for me.

Discussion Questions

1. What are some barriers that keep Christians from plugging into the ultimate power source, Jesus Christ?
2. When barriers arise that keep you from plugging into Jesus' power source, what are some strategies to help you stay plugged in?
3. Name two or three scriptures you can use as reminders that Jesus is our power source and strength.
4. What is your definition of brokenness?
5. What has been the glue in your life when everything was falling apart?

Lesson Learned - "Plugged Into the Source - Jesus Christ"

CHAPTER 2

GOD ALLOWED IT!

I believe circumstances and situations that occur in my life were allowed to happen by God. He allowed my divorce to happen. It was my husband's choice to divorce me. Could God have stopped my divorce? Yes, He could have, but God gives each person the right to make his or her own decisions, right or wrong. We are not robots. One of the most tough lessons I had to deal with was that God allowed this trial to come into my life. It's as if I can hear the devil challenging God, "Let's see how Marlene comes out of this one." I know that God assured Satan that Marlene would stand on the Word of God and lean on His everlasting arms. While I understand God wasn't the cause of my divorce, He granted me the strength to persevere through the challenges set before me. Throughout this journey, I've faced moments of uncertainty and stumbled numerous times, but I never completely lost my footing.

In the beginning, I was so offended that God allowed this extreme trial to come into my life. I wasn't angry with God, just offended. One does not have a right to be offended with God.

Please let me be transparent! In my finite mind, I thought there were so many other lessons God could have taught me, with other trial scenarios. Please, not this trial Lord. I know I cannot choose my trials, and I cannot outrule God. Pride is spoken about in Proverbs 16:18 which says "Pride goeth before destruction, and a haughty spirit before a fall." I didn't tell God what to do, but this trial hurts! It really hurts. God is sovereign; I knew this in theory and practice, but it hurt when His sovereignty affected me in such a way.

Songs of Pain and Purpose

Carol Antrom, a Christian composer, and a former high school classmate and friend of mine at Overbrook High School, wrote the song "Sovereign." Her song speaks exactly to my situation. Because of who God is, He doesn't have to answer to no one.

I just could not believe that God would let this trial of a divorce happen to me. I've consistently upheld the principles of Christian living, striving to lead a holy life. Tithing, serving the Lord, maintaining daily personal devotions, teaching and empowering my public middle school students, and treating my family, neighbors, and friends with kindness. And even with all this, I had to learn that I had to fit into His plan. God also shines on the just and the unjust. Is this powerful or what? Carol Antrom also wrote another song entitled "Stand Still," which was recorded by Rev. Ernest Davis and the Wilmington-Chester Mass Choir. While in my valley experience, I stood still and waited for God to speak His will to me.

As David states in the first part of Psalm 55:4, "My heart is severely pained within me." There was a feeling and pain in my heart that would not go away. Through the passage of time and the comfort of the Holy Spirit, my hurting soul was slowly being healed. The Lord is a healer and a comforter. Through the course of time, I have been able to forgive my former husband, and I have moved on without bitterness in my heart. This forgiveness was a gradual process; time is a healer. At the beginning of my journey, I didn't think forgiveness was possible, and it further stands as a testament to God's hand upon my life. I walk this journey one day at a time!

When you ask, "Why me, Lord?" God might answer, "Why not you?" This trial is not about you. For example, Mary, the mother of Jesus, had to experience the painful trial of watching her son be crucified on that horrible cross. They crucified Jesus on the cross, died, and rose again in three days to cancel the sting of death for all of us. This was His assignment, not his mother's assignment. The angel Gabriel didn't give Mary the crucifixion story when he told her she would conceive, bear a son, and call him Jesus. Jesus Christ's purpose for coming to the earth was to die – to cancel the sting of death and be our sacrificial lamb. The crucifixion of Christ had to be completed. It wasn't about Mary having to watch her son die on the cross; her son dying on the cross was about you and me. Jesus had to die to give us the opportunity to have eternal life through Jesus Christ (John 3:16).

Throughout my separation and divorce, my family and friends, church family members, colleagues, acquaintances, and neighbors were witnesses as I went through the valley. It was like they were saying, "How will this God, whom Marlene sings about, talks about, testifies about, and prays to, help her in this situation?" Well, it was extremely difficult, and like Mary, I still didn't know my entire story. I had to lean on every scripture that I ever knew, studied, and memorized. Hymns of the faith and Sunday School and Christian summer camp songs that I hadn't sung in years came to my memory. While in the valley, these songs helped sustain and comfort me.

Place great hymns of the faith and songs inside of you. A fictitious rhythm and blues song, "Do it to Me Baby," could not possibly help me now. No secular lyrics could have possibly sustained or comforted my grieving spirit; in fact, they may actually have created more conflict in my spirit. But the hymns and scriptures left me no doubt that God proved Himself over and over to me. The hurt I experienced during my difficult walk was very painful. The more I allowed the hymns to minister to my spirit, the more I knew I had to rely solely on His Power, His Word, and His Promises.

God's Promises

A few of God's Words and promises:

1. "The Lord is my shepherd; I shall not want." Psalm 23:1
2. "For thou art with me." Psalm 23:4b
3. "If you ask any thing in my name, I will do it." John 14:14
4. "The Lord is our keeper." "The Lord shall preserve thee from all evil." Psalm 121:5a&7
5. "My help cometh from the Lord." Psalm 121:2

During and after the divorce, those scriptures gave me the boldness to move beyond grief and help other women with comfort, prayer, and a word from the Lord while they navigated their own trials (including divorce). I told one of my dear sisters-in-the-Lord that if the Lord's plan was for me to go through my divorce to help her, it was worth it. Therefore, people who are in pain can often feel the pain of others.

Prayerfully, others gained strength as they saw God working in my life. Testimonies are so powerful. Some testimonies aren't always spoken, but people watch the lives of other people as they go through a life experience.

When I look back over my life and think of all the trials and tribulations I have been through, I know I am truly blessed. I've got a testimony! Through it all, I tried to be joyful and praise

God. I wasn't always successful. Nevertheless, I didn't want to let God down. I knew He was counting on me to live out the Word of God. I knew others were rooting for me, too.

You may wonder, did I say, "Why Me?" Yes, I asked myself repeatedly, "Why me?" It was not until years later that I knew "why me." God had given me my assignment, which was to go through this valley experience. We do not all have the same assignment; each assignment has its own set of variables and circumstances, which are unique to each person. I called upon the Lord and He showed me great and mighty things (Jeremiah 33:3).

Good or bad, we can learn from every lesson. This learned lesson helped me to not focus on myself. As it was to be, one of my friend's husbands asked her for a divorce during the same time period as my divorce trial. I could minister and pray for her through my learned lessons and painful life experiences, because this was not about me, but about using me to help others.

I heard the Lord say, "Marlene, I have a news flash for you! This trial is NOT about you. You may think the trial is about you, but it is not."

This lesson helped me focus on how to go through the trial. Yes, I believe I had been wronged; in my head I said, "Marlene, retaliate and make yourself feel great." Vengeance feels good, but God says, "Vengeance is mine; I will repay, saith the Lord" The instructions in Romans 12:19 state, "Dearly beloved, avenge not yourselves, but rather give place unto wrath: for it is written, Vengeance is mine; I will repay, saith the Lord." So if you enter a vengeance mode against your attackers, God will judge you and make you accountable for all your wrongful actions. Then you will be punished God's way. Trust me; it is not worth it. Heed the warning.

Your trial is the vehicle to your new understanding of God's will and how He can operate in your life. There are lessons to be learned while going through difficult times. If you are smart, learn the lessons the first time, so that you do not have to learn that same lesson over and over again. Spiritual Summer School for those persons who flunk is not fun. Learn while walking through the first time.

Another lesson I learned while in the midst of this experience is that someone is watching your story. My then-husband had already informed certain church leaders and members of the church about his decision to leave me. Consequently, when those congregants who were aware of the situation saw me, their expressions were filled with sorrowful eyes. Can you imagine attending a place of worship where some people thought they knew your story?

Some of my friends asked me why I didn't open the door for him since he wanted to leave. They also felt as though I should have told him to pack his bags or literally help him pack his bags when he mentioned he was going to leave. Believe it or not, he stayed two more years before permanently leaving the home. Please don't judge me! My choice to allow him to stay was based on what I thought was the right thing to do at that time.

During this time, I still ministered in area churches as the pianist, choir director, and soloist, and functioned as a good minister's wife despite what was going on. Again, please don't judge me. God told me to be a good wife, be nice to him, show kindness, and wait to see what the end would be. I hoped he would stay in the marriage, but the handwriting was on the wall.

My children saw the interaction between us, and it affected their lives, too. During a separation and divorce process, children are often a casualty of war. No matter what the research has stated, or public opinion on divorce, my children can never say that I threw their father out of their home!

. . .

Someone is Watching Your Story

I often felt sad for Diana, Princess of Wales, who had to suffer going through a separation and divorce and even die in a car crash, with the entire whole wide world watching her pain and agony. But God is able. I can testify that you can walk through victoriously while many are watching your pain. God will help you through it all!

There are two things that I would not wish on my worst enemy: a caesarean birth and/or a divorce. Although I went through both situations, I feel there are so many other types of trials one could go through to learn biblical lessons. Each of us will go through different tests. Unfortunately, we don't get the opportunity to choose the tests or timing, nor what types of lessons we will go through.

I am not sure how God assessed me for my actions and behavior while going through my separation and divorce. I do not know what grade I will receive for my actions while going through my separation and divorce. Did God give me a midterm grade at the halfway mark of my valley experience? All I knew was that God was my strength and my help (Psalm 27:1). God's strength helped me keep going! "I press toward the mark for the prize of the high calling of God in Christ Jesus." (Philippians 3:14). Yes Lord!

When my husband stated he wanted out of the marriage, as I wrote earlier, I cursed him with a few choice words. I received an "F" for failing that test. Why didn't I just quietly quote and bless him with scripture and an encouraging Word from the Lord? This may have been a good time to give him a word of prophecy. Tough times bring out some "stuff" we didn't know we had inside of us. God just showed me the darker side of myself. I had cursed no one before until that moment. I offer no excuse for my actions.

After my five minutes of insanity, I was back on the right track. Attacked, misused, misled, and misguided are a few of the emotions I felt; however, at that very time, I didn't realize this trial was not about me. Marlene, get it through your head! Get rid of all those "I's." This is not about you!

I believe God was actually glorified in my separation and divorce. Did you just faint? Are you picking yourself off the floor? Yes, it's true. I believe God was glorified in my separation and divorce. Give Him glory; give Him praise! My painful experience has helped other women and men go through their experiences just a little easier. If God can do it for me and for others, He can do it for you, too. The Lord has given me opportunities to minister to women and men during their tough times. My journey was not about me. I was not the only one going through or to have gone through a divorce. Praise be to God that I walked through the valley experience with my head held high and with my mind intact! Praise the Lord!

Discussion Questions

1. Do you believe God's will is perfect and we must accept and deal with it?
2. Do you wish you had the power to change the course of your life according to your perception?
3. If you could rewrite one chapter of your life, what chapter would choose to change?
4. Although life hands us lemons at times, how can you turn your valley experience into a learning experience?
5. Reflect on one of your valley experiences. Who was encouraged by your testimony or story of how God helped you with your trial?
6. How difficult is it for you not to focus on your trial, but be intentional on your reactions, attitudes, and demeanor while in a valley experience?

Lesson Learned - "God Allowed It"

CHAPTER 3

TEST, TRIALS, AND TRIBULATIONS

Some of what seem to be our trials and tribulations aren't trials and tribulations at all. Many are only tests. All I know is that trials, tribulations, and tests have many variables in common. Each one is painful and each one starts with a "T." At some point in your Christian walk or just in life, you will experience all three.

Disobedience to God's Word brings about chastisement. Chastisement brings about painful punishments that can be manifested in many forms. God chooses the punishment and the degree and level. My Momma said, "If you play with fire, you will get burnt." There are consequences for our actions.

I have also realized that the consequences of sin not only affect the one who has sinned, but many times it can affect an entire group of people connected to them.

In my heart, I know I wasn't single-handedly responsible for my divorce. Of course, I must remove my angelic halo and take some responsibility for the demise of my marriage. Everyone has an opinion, and my former husband surely has his own opinions about our marriage too, but God holds the record. And that is what counts! To move forward, I confessed known and unknown sin where my marriage was concerned. I just wanted a clean heart and to be in right fellowship before the Lord.

Trials, tribulations, and tests are a part of my personal testimony. Have you ever noticed that the word "test" is the first four letters of the word testimony? When you come out of your trials, tests, and tribulations, you will have a testimony. Some people are reading your testimony as you go through without you giving a formal declaration of what is going on in your life. I have a testimony!

What is your testimony? Is it connected to being in a situation where people are using you in a hurtful manner? Does it require you to frequently practice forgiveness and turn the other cheek? Is there a constant reminder to leave the business of vengeance to God? Can you believe God loves our adversaries? How could God wrap His arms around my husband, who has turned my life upside down? God also loves the employer, neighbor, church member in your auxiliary (club), co-worker, and/or stranger who makes your life miserable. Believe it or not, Jesus died on Calvary for them, too. The people who make our lives miserable or difficult can make or break us. You will either be victorious through your trial(s) or you will fail miserably. The blessing is that your trial will not last forever.

Is it difficult to believe and accept that it is possible for God to love, forgive, and shine favor on your adversaries? Matthew 5:45 talks about this very same thing. "That ye may be the children of your Father, which is in heaven: for He maketh his sun to rise on the evil and on the good, and sendeth rain on the just and on the unjust."

This concept is hard for some to understand and accept. (Pray for me!) Why would God bless a person who has caused so much pain? God shines on the just and the unjust. Remember, "Vengeance is mine; I will repay, saith the Lord" (Romans 12:19).

So I am waiting for the Lord to take care of my situation. We must let go of some things. I am a work-in-process. God died for everyone, no matter who they are or what they have done to others.

I don't care how other people define divorce. My definition is: Divorce is war! The legal court documents state "plaintiff versus defendant." One person versus another; spouse A versus spouse B. In my opinion, this defines war.

It is important that we forgive our adversaries. Remember, God has forgiven us. We mustn't overlook or trivialize what they have done to us. God looks at our reactions and behavior in the situation, and we are held accountable for everything we say and do. I still cannot believe I went to the dark side of myself when I was asked for a divorce. Temporary insanity works in the court of law, but not with God. Wrongful, horrific, and awful things may happen to you, but it is up to you to do what is right before God. Life is not fair! The unfairness of life hurts. God is concerned with our responses, attitudes, reactions, and actions in response to what happens to us.

Although there are books on the divorce process, I did not know of any classes on how to go through a divorce. (I now know of Christian support groups for those who are separated, divorcing, and divorced.) Nobody prepares for this time of life, or do they? Does anyone say, "When my spouse separates and divorces me, I will do this and then do that." I didn't have a plan, and I lacked direction.

My perfected body does not come about until I get to heaven. Please be patient with me; God is not through with me yet. It is a blessing to know that God forgives. Since God forgives, we are called to do the same towards others. My faith has been tested. The lessons I learned while walking through the fire were invaluable to my journey.

Discussion Questions

1. What scriptures from the Bible give the assurance that God forgives sins if we confess them?
2. Why does God love your adversary? What scriptural support can you find for your answer? Is that fair? Why or why not?
3. Why did Jesus die on the cross?
4. Name at least three adversaries of Jesus. What was His response or attitude towards them?
5. What should our godly response be towards those who are against us?

LESSON LEARNED – "TEST, TRIALS, AND TRIBULATIONS"

CHAPTER 4

GOD KNOWS THE ENDING

God is Alpha and Omega (Revelations 1:8). God knew me before I was formed in my mother's belly, knows the number of hairs on my head, and knows each stage of my life before it happens. The devil does not know my future; only God knows. Our friends and families don't know the ending to our story either.

During my time as the praise and worship leader at a local Philadelphia church, one of my favorite songs to lead was entitled "He Knows My Name." God knows precisely how my life and yours will unfold. The events in my life are no surprise to Him and the same holds true for your life as well. What a blessing to know that God has and will take care of me. He will take good care of you, too. Share your thoughts and feelings with God because He wants to hear from us, and I enjoy doing just that, too. Give it to God; He'll bear it. Don't try to alter God's plan. Walk the journey. Ask the Savior to help you, for there is nothing that God cannot handle.

There is a debate in Christendom about God's permissive will versus God's divine will. God's divine will is His predestined or exact plan for our lives; God's permissive will is what He will allow or permit one to do in life. I don't believe we will receive all that God has for us when we do our own thing. Some Christians believe we can ask God to change His will for us, and others feel we are unable to ask or change God's will or plan for us. Can we change either? We can debate this forever. I cannot change my circumstances, but I can be watchful of my response to my difficult circumstances.

Beginning at sixteen, I started composing songs. Little did I know that those early-composed songs that flowed from my fingers would continue to speak to me in my adult life while in the valley. During my wedding in 1981, my church's Rosebud Children's Choir, for which I was the pianist and choral director, sang a selection I composed entitled "Let the Lord Lead You." The Lord knew before I spoke the words "I do" at our marriage ceremony how my life would look way down the road. The song speaks about life's journey and taking God by the hand, because He holds the Master Plan. Who knew that twenty years later our marriage would officially end? One verse from the above song states:

> Even though storms of life may come your way
> Even though the storms of life
> Look like they'll never stop coming down
> The Word of God stands true.
> He will never
> No, no ever
> Forsake His children, just believe on Him.

© 1979 Marlene Jenkins Cooper

I am not a prophetess, but those words rang true and were manifested in my life many years later. On the journey, I stumbled, but God picked me up as I tried to follow Him. My path often seemed dark during this time period, but God shined the light and led me all the way.

During this time, I had to sing and meditate on the written words of the song I composed twenty-five years prior to the divorce. God has never forsaken His children, I can testify. I praise Him for his loving arms wrapped all around me.

How would I react to my life if God showed me upfront His entire plan for my life, with all the experiences? Or how would I have lived my married life if God had shared all the experiences of my marriage before I got married? Unfortunately, life does not work like this. Each day is a new day with new life experiences. What happened during the marriage only strengthened me and made me wiser. Lots of lessons were learned. God said I should trust Him with all my heart and lean not to my own understanding. If I acknowledge Him, He will direct my path (Proverbs 3:5 & 6). His Word stands true! God directed the pathways of my life and led me to a holy place.

Although my marriage is over, the rest of my life's story is still being written. Life goes on. I don't know the ending, but God does. I can rest in Him and live my life! The Bible states in Jeremiah 29:11, "For I know the thoughts that I think toward you, saith the Lord, thoughts of peace, and not of evil, to give you an expected end."

FRIENDS UNTIL THE END?

Don't expect your friends to walk the entire journey with you. I didn't learn this lesson on my own. A guest speaker, a pastor's wife, gave the listeners forewarning about this topic during a lecture about her own life experiences of betrayal and divorce. Some of her friendships ended during her divorce, but she understood why. She stated that not all of your friends can continue the journey with you.

During my journey, some of my friends departed the friendship. Although I could surmise why they could not go the distance with me, I still felt the pain of abandonment. Didn't they know that I needed their friendship and support during this difficult season in my life? How could some of my friends leave me high and dry? This could not be happening to me. Some of my close friends departed too. Spoiler alert! Some friends will go the distance, and then they may drop off. Certain friends will pray and fast on your behalf, but if God takes too long to fix your problem, they may leave the scene too. This does not mean that all of your friends will leave the friendship. Thank God for the friends that can and will go the distance. Some people have problems of their own and cannot always focus on helping you.

Some of your friends may leave the friendship while you are experiencing difficult times. Don't fret; God is able to give you added friends, or you may have to walk and rely on God by yourself. Remember the race isn't given to the swift. Endure to the end! Read Ecclesiastes 9:11.

One of my closest friends of many years chose to leave our friendship during the time of my separation and divorce. I am not clear on the reason or reasons why. Since I was fighting for my life, sanity, and emotional stability, I didn't feel the need to ask her about it. Then again, everyone makes choices. I never called her and whined about my marital situation. Maybe she thought bad times, separation, and divorce were a disease that was contagious. Although I am saddened to have lost the close friendship of one of my sisters-in-Christ, my heavenly Father has put others in my life.

Jesus spoke to the disciples, as recorded in John 14:18: "I will not leave you comfortless: I will come to you." Jesus knew what it meant to not to depend on friends. When He was in the Garden of Gethsemane in deep anguish, He asked His disciples to pray with Him. The disciples were just too tired and fell asleep. Why could Jesus' disciples not sit and pray with Him for a little while?

Many friends mean well, but not all will stay the course with you until the end. Will friends stick closer than a brother or sister during a trial? If your trial takes too long to victoriously come to an end, some of your best friends might drop off. It is challenging for people to walk others through their issues, especially when they are grappling with their own troubles.

Even my mother left me for a time at the beginning of my valley experience. My whole situation was so horrific that my mother internalized my problem. The family doctor surmised that some situation caused her blood pressure to escalate and her nerves to be on edge. David's inspired words from God in Psalm 27:10 helped me with my situation. The Psalm states, "When my father and my mother forsake me, then the Lord will take me up." Although I trusted the Lord to handle my trial, my body didn't feel so well either; so I also went to see my family doctor. We all had the same doctor. Our doctor, who is a family friend, surmised that something was wrong with the Jenkins-Cooper family. Each one of us saw him on separate occasions. He put two and two together and figured out something was wrong. "Is there something wrong with your daughter?" he asked my mother before he treated the symptoms. She responded in a quiet voice, "Yes." Although I needed her emotional support, my mother didn't leave me of her own free will; she had to physically get better. After a very short while, Momma was back. Stress is not nice!

The Family of God

During the entire journey, where was my church family, with whom I spent eighteen years in ministry and membership? Where were the encouraging notes, hugs of understanding, comforting words, and prayers? While in my brokenness, the membership and church leadership smiled and walked right past me each Sunday. Some knew and others did not. Two years prior to our separation, my former husband communicated to some of the leadership of the church that he was divorcing me. My childhood friend and ministry partner at church often prayed with me about my life's circumstances. Another member, who was a long-time family friend, came to our house when he found out my husband wanted to leave the family. He came to talk and pray with him about his decision to leave the home and divorce his wife. I praise God for both people, who were the only church members of my home church, who prayed and reached out to us. (Many years later, I found out that one of the ministers prayed with my former husband about his decision to divorce me.) They didn't come to our home as official representatives of our church but as our friends. Nonetheless, I was blessed by their involvement in our lives.

Frequently during Sunday worship services at our home church, I sat on the front row on the right side of the church with my husband. During the offering period, while I was in the front row, I shook the hands of the parishioners as they gave their offerings and filed past me. (In many African-American Baptist churches, parishioners shake the hands of the leadership after they give their tithes and offerings and return to their seats.) Normally, I would have been with the choir, but because of the circumstances of my marriage, I resigned as choir director. My husband was one of the associate ministers of the church and also played the organ, which was near the first pew in the church. I could have sat on the last pew of the sanctuary of the church and worshipped the Lord, but I sat with him on the front pew. In my brokenness, I smiled and shook the hands of the people and struggled to worship the Lord.

Although some of the church leadership of my then-home church knew of my plight, no one said a word to me. Could I get a prayer, a card, a hug, and/or an encouraging word from anyone? I would have welcomed the church mice to encourage me or state that they were praying for me. I asked for a meeting and was granted one with some pastors and church leadership. When I shared my feelings of abandonment from the leadership of the church during my pending separation from one of their ministers, one of the leadership members chided me for going to the senior pastor. A member of the joint board made a recommendation that I go to counseling to become a better wife and mother. Really? Are you serious? I attended counseling sessions with a woman counselor from the church's counseling team. After a while, I decided no thanks and stopped the sessions.

What was I thinking? Maybe I should not have called a meeting with the leadership. I am not bitter against the leadership; however, I was extremely offended. Who was I supposed to go to in the church about my marital situation? Was I supposed to go to the woman at the end of the ninth row and tell her about one of their church's associate ministers and ask for prayer? Maybe I could have addressed this with the wives of the ministers and pastors and told them of my plight. There was no plan or rulebook to help me with these questions. I did what I thought was right in my own eyes.

I trust I will never travel this road again. Although I went through a marital divorce, I felt that my church divorced me as well. My former husband had been a member of that church since he was five years old, but I was there for eighteen years. The pain of abandonment by some of the members was immense. My "church hurt" was real. My former church family will never know how much they hurt and disappointed me during my valley experience. When I removed my church membership after my husband left me, my children and I never heard from any of the members of that church. Maybe I thought too highly of myself to get a call from someone.

In the past, that church was very supportive of my family. When my husband went on business trips, the former Chairman of the Deacon Board would drive past my house and go through my driveway to make sure all was well while my husband was away. If the former Chairman of the Deacon Board had been alive during my valley experience, I wondered how he would have handled this entire situation with my family.

My family had a Christian overnight camp in Lake Lure, North Carolina. The church membership supported the camp by sending their children, giving monetary gifts, and offering prayers. Many of the church members were even staff members. To this day, I still love the people of my former church; I talk to them and attend special services and funerals. God has healed my hurt of abandonment through the test of time.

"We are family!" was my former church's motto and was printed on the back of the Sunday bulletin each Sunday. Where were the church family's love, compassion, kindheartedness, and concern for me? I was a church family member and a part of the music team! Minister to those who you know who are hurting the next time you see a fellow church member or friend going through a difficult time. Although this may be difficult for many people, extend yourself and send a card or text message. Pray for them and/or give an encouraging hug. One cannot take away another's pain or make things better, but one can show love and support. Stand with them if you can. I felt so alone at my former church. I guess my divorce included my church as well.

As stated earlier, we do not know who will be there for us during difficult times. God put others in place who gave me a hug, sent me a card, and gave encouraging words. I just thought my church family would have been there for me during this time.

I am sure others would have handled this entire situation

differently. Some would have left that church and found a new one. Others may have stayed home from church and not attended at all. No matter what others may have done, I chose to stay at that church until I felt God leading me to do differently.

We must rely on God for what we need. People may disappoint or disillusion us. We must trust God for what we need and let Him meet our needs. The song "Encourage Yourself!" composed by the prolific songwriter Donald Lawrence helped me do just that. I had to give myself what I needed. Although many of my close friends and family were also there to help me during this ordeal, from time-to-time, I still had to encourage myself.

I was asked for a divorce on January 17, 1997. He left the family home on February 1, 1999, and the divorce was completed on July 31, 2003. This six-year time period was a very long time. Remember, not everyone will walk with you during your trial if God takes a long while to deliver you from your trials and tribulations. Praise God for the friends who have the stamina and courage to stick with you during your most difficult times.

Remember, God's timing differs from ours. His time is not our time (Isaiah 55:8). Friends mean well, but if you aren't delivered from your situation in a timely manner, some friends and family may move on. There is a season for everything. Although hurt feelings may occur if your friends cannot walk with you during the entire journey, rely on Jesus to heal those hurts. Just like the weather, some friends are seasonal. This statement may sound hurtful, but it is true. Not all of your friendships will last a lifetime. Don't let this be upsetting to you! For everything, there is a season. Ecclesiastes 9:11 says, "I returned, and saw under the sun, that the race is not to the swift, nor the battle to the strong, neither yet bread to the wise, nor yet riches to men of understanding, nor yet favour to men of skill; but time and chance happeneth to them all."

God is omnipotent, all-powerful. He will endure with you to the end. That is why we lean and depend on Jesus. He is our help! The author of Psalm 121:2 says, "My help cometh from the Lord, which made heaven and earth."

Jesus, accompanied by his disciples, went to the garden to pray. He said to them, "My soul is exceeding sorrowful, even unto death: tarry ye here, watch with me" (Matthew 26:38). The disciples of Jesus loved Him very much. Nevertheless, they could not stand and pray with Him because they were physically exhausted. If the disciples could not stand and pray with Jesus during His roughest hour, what makes you think all your friends can watch, pray, and stand with you? Remember, the spirit is willing, but the flesh is weak (Matthew 26:41).

Prayerfully, most of your friends will not leave you "hanging" by yourself. You may meet new friends and/or gain new prayer partners to walk with you. Or you may be so blessed to have all your close friends stand with you. When some of your friendships dissipate, please understand why. However, you will never guess which ones will walk with you until the end.

The word divorce is a powerful word that evokes all kinds of emotions. I believe one of my friends just dropped me as a friend because she thought divorce was a contagious disease. I just wanted to be made whole, have my pain eradicated, and feel normal again. Praise be to God for the friends who had the stamina and courage to stick with me during my most difficult life trial.

Being a friend to one who is going through a hard trial or tribulation is a lot of work. We expect a friend to listen to us ramble on, cry with us, take us out to dinner to forget what is really happening to us, pray unceasingly, fast with us, offer support and encouragement, and just sit and be with us. This is asking a great deal of people, with no time frame or promise of an ending date, but God is a keeper.

Can you stand with your sister or brother-in-Christ and still have your own issues? It can be done, but it is trying, painful, distressful, and stressful, though rewarding. I was blessed to have a core of friends who listened to me ramble on and on about the same thing over and over. My litany was as follows: "I was married for twenty years. I believe I was a good wife and mother. And I cannot believe…How could he?" To my sisters and brothers-in-Christ who stuck with me during this time period, a million thanks! Galatians 6:2 talks about bearing one another's burdens. It states, "Bear ye one another's burdens, and so fulfill the law of Christ."

I was also blessed to be apart of a city-wide minister and pastor's wives class who met once a week to talk about their roles in the church. When the ladies heard of my plight, these ladies were very supportive. They prayed and encouraged me while I was in the valley. One of them fasted on my behalf. I was ever so grateful to the teachers and ladies of the class.

Most of my friends who stood with me during this time were women; however, my childhood friend and best man at our wedding was one of my most encouraging male friends. He mailed a card of encouragement to me that was very supportive. He periodically visited my family and my parents to check on us. On certain occasions, he visited my son's church, which was down the street from his pastorate, and warmly greeted him and gave him a few dollars. While he was having his own problems, he overlooked them and helped us. While one may argue that it is his responsibility as a minister and pastor to shepherd others, my family members were not part of his congregation. We are immensely grateful for his enduring friendship of over five decades.

Another male friend of the family periodically called to

check on us. I'm thankful to my girlfriend who allowed her husband to call me while I was in the valley.

    Be grateful for the ones who can walk with you and understand why the others cannot go the distance. God knows the ending. He is there for you. Others may get weary, but God will remain true to you and will walk with you while you are in the valley. Only some may go the distance with you, but Jesus will always be there. Remember, you have a friend in Jesus.

Discussion Questions

1. Given that some trials can persist for years, would you like to know the ending if you could? Please share your reasons.
2. Just for fun, rewrite a particular time in your life. Describe how you would have ideally wanted it to end. Dream on.
3. What Bible verses can provide you with strength and comfort during an extended period of trial?
4. How has this chapter encouraged you to give some type of support (a card, act of kindness, phone call, hug, an encouraging text message, prayer with them, etc.) to those you know who are hurting in your family, church, and/or community? Is there someone specific who may need your encouragement at this time?
5. Have you ever experienced a lack of support from friends or family during challenging times, and how did you manage without their help?

Lesson Learned – "God Knows The Ending"

CHAPTER 5

WALKING AND LIVING THE WORD

Do you have a favorite book of the Bible, or a favorite verse? Before I walked through this most recent valley experience, the Old Testament book of Psalms was my favorite book of the Bible. During this time, I learned to grab hold of Scripture verses and review them often. Isaiah, the Old Testament prophet, didn't know about me when he wrote the book of Isaiah, but God inspired him to write it, knowing that Marlene Jenkins Cooper would need to stand on verses written by him through the inspiration of God. The book of Isaiah is now my favorite book of the Bible.

Isaiah has become one of my favorite prophets, books of the Bible, and male names. I inadvertently called one of my most disruptive students Isaiah instead of his real name Israel. I am not sure why I would continue to do this. However, because of my love for the book of Isaiah in the Bible, I would try to understand and encourage this wayward student to do better. It was an uphill battle, and I didn't succeed while he was at my school.

The following scriptures in Isaiah helped me along while in the valley:

Isaiah 26:3
"Thou wilt keep him in perfect peace, whose mind is stayed on thee: because he trusteth in thee."

Ministers and pastors often state to those they are ministering to that other people have lost their minds going through what they have gone through. I am so blessed that I was able to keep my mind stayed on Jehovah and let Him hold my hand and walk me through. The Lord inspired me to compose a song based on this scripture entitled "Perfect Peace."

Verse 2 of Isaiah 43 resonated in my heart as I experienced difficult times. "When thou passest through the waters, I will be with thee; and through the rivers, they shall not overflow thee: when thou walkest through the fire, thou shalt not be burned; neither shall the flame kindle upon thee." I have walked through the high waters; gone through the eye of the flames, and the Lord has kept me. The pain from the flames was great, but the Lord kept me. The pain that I felt in my heart only could be eased and soothed by the balm in Gilead, Jesus Himself.

Isaiah 54:17
"No weapon that is formed against thee shall prosper; and every tongue that shall rise against you in judgment you thou shall condemn. This is the heritage of the servants of the Lord, and their righteousness is of me, says the Lord."

Another verse that helped me immensely is Joel 2:25, "And I will restore to you the years that the locust hath eaten, the cankerworm, and the caterpillar, and the palmerworm, my great army which I sent among you."

I praise the Lord and I am ever so grateful that I did not become as financially destitute as some have while going through a divorce. Many divorced women have taken a financial hit because of a separation and/or divorce due to the loss of their husband's income. The Lord has blessed my children and me in that we didn't have to move into a women's shelter, move in with my parents, cease extracurricular and after-school activities, and/or discontinue the dreams of attending college for either of my children.

I created a curriculum called "Life 101" for young people (grades 6-8) to experience fifty years of living from 18–68 years of age in a 12-week computer course. In one of my middle school Life 101 classes, my students' assignment was to revise their fictitious, married-with-two-children budget spreadsheet to that of single-parenthood-with-two-children budget-spreadsheet, because of the loss of a spouse because of divorce or death. The students agonized over their spreadsheets to achieve a workable budget. Many of them could not! They told me they have to move back home and live with their parents in order to have a workable budget. Many could not afford their houses, cars, hairdresser appointments, or even childcare. In real life situations, this happens daily to adults who have to make those tough decisions. Life for my students became real! Their budgets had to balance out in order to receive a passing grade!

During this time, besides my full-time job, I worked six side jobs. My jobs included work at every school extracurricular activity for which I was possibly qualified, and some for which I wasn't. I was even the cheerleading coach! What skills did I have to be the cheerleading coach? Absolutely none! I did not even make the color guard team in high school. The students begged me to take the position because their previous coach was promoted to another position within the Health, Safety, and Physical Education Department and was sent to the Central Office. Well, with the help of my student cheerleaders and my tenacity, we won multiple awards for our participation in contests.

Additionally, I also was the organist/pianist/choir director/praise and worship director for many churches. Yes, I was tired from working all of my jobs, but I did love what I was doing. I had to give up a few jobs, too. For example, volleyball coaching was one of them. After all, a mom can only work so much and raise two children by herself!

All of my jobs, in addition to my primary job, and creative budgeting allowed me to become debt-free while going through my separation and divorce. In 2003, except for the mortgage on my home, I was debt-free. I wished I were able to scream, "I'm debt-free!" on the *Dave Ramsey Show*.

During the year that my daughter Joy became a junior at Harvard University and my son Mark entered Hampton University as a freshman, my finances became super challenged. It was my choice to allow my children to attend the private universities of their choice. The financial impact of their college education challenged me for many years. Credit cards, a large Parent Plus loan, and scholarships assisted me with financing their college education; however, I would advise no one to finance their children's college education with credit cards and governmental Parent Plus loans. But God! He is faithful to do exceedingly, abundantly more than I can ask or think (Ephesians 3:20). When the Lord states He will restore you, He will. In later years, Jesus restored my finances, a broken heart, and a broken spirit. Praise The Lord!

God speaks to His children through Scripture, circumstances, people, songs, prayer, and His Spirit. Listening to the voice of God is mind-boggling. One needs to have a relationship with God to hear His voice. His voice was not audible to me, but I heard the Lord speak clearly to me during the time of the break-up of my marriage. As I fasted, read my Bible, and prayed, God gave me three words: stand, love, and forgive. I heard these three words from the Lord and told Him I could do all three with no problem. Yes Lord! I am with you. Before you tell God the Father that you can do what He asks, get all the facts first.

I was made aware of some information about my marriage, which caused me to delay forgiveness for my husband. Okay, Lord! Maybe forgiving my husband will take a little more time. That time frame took an additional eleven years. Be honest with yourself; if you aren't ready to forgive, ask God for help with being able to release someone and yourself through forgiveness. Trying to be super spiritual is one thing, but God knows your heart.

The Lord asked me to forgive my husband. I said, "Okay Lord, but I am waiting for an apology from him." Every summer, my church sponsors a "Completely Yes" women's conference. This particular year it was in Lancaster, Pennsylvania. While attending the conference, I received a breakthrough and could honestly forgive him for what I believed he did against me. This time period was an extremely long time from the time of my divorce decree. Forgiveness came from my heart. I learned to free myself and forgive him without an apology.

God also speaks to us through prayer time with Him. My godly parents taught their children to pray daily and unceasingly, so I knew how to pray from the time I was a little girl. The Apostle Paul writes in First Thessalonians 5:17, "Pray without ceasing." At this point, I had been a praying Christian woman for nearly thirty years. I was one who had personal daily devotions with God; nonetheless, during this particularly difficult time in my life, I learned the value and necessity of a great prayer life.

During my valley experience, as I walked through my classroom at school, I constantly kept in touch with Jesus. As I walked from student to student, I was silently praying for help, direction, guidance, and intervention from God for my personal life. My middle school students didn't have a clue what I was doing or going through my personal life. I wasn't chanting or moving my lips or going to some ethereal place as I taught, but in every free moment, I was in silent prayer. There is a line from an old-time hymn of the church, "Yield Not to Temptation" by Horatio R. Palmer, that states, "Just ask the Savior to help you." God wants to and will help us! Our Lord and Savior wants to help you in times of trouble and pain, and He is there for us! Thank you, Jesus! I praise God for His help, love, support, and comfort.

When my former husband decided he was physically leaving on that particular day, I could not call out sick from my job because of the horrible news just given to me. I went to work and educated my students. When he first asked for a divorce, I could not take an extended leave of absence from work and all of my responsibilities and stay in bed until the horrific experience was over. It is hilarious that some of my students would often inform me that my enthusiasm for the subject matter and over-the-top actions weren't necessary to teach a lesson or concept. When I gave them the boring, dull teacher voice, they quickly changed their mind. I am ever so thankful to God that I was able to effectively teach my students, even while my heartaches were so painful. If they only knew…….

Pray Without Ceasing

Praying without ceasing is not only praying aloud, but also being in tune with God and communicating with God. During this period in my life, I heard God speak to me. The Holy Spirit comforted my soul. He walked me through this period in my life. The Word of God is powerful and true. As I look back over my life, I see that the Lord has been good to me and I have been so blessed. I can testify!

God will give you a word when you need it. During my valley experience, I found myself always looking for "a Word" from the Lord. My soul craved to hear the Lord speak to me during this time of pain and suffering. "Speak, Lord; for thy servant heareth" (First Samuel 3:9). I would look and listen for a

"Word from the Lord" in the Bible, in personal devotions, from sermons given by men and women of God, in Christian songs, and in the testimonies of others.

Although I faithfully attended Sunday morning worship services during this time, I found no solace or comfort at my home church. Therefore, I read the Bible, went to revivals in the Philadelphia area, and watched Trinity Broadcasting Network (TBN) for my spiritual renewal. My family and some of my friends were concerned that I was listening to televangelists who weren't preaching the correct Word of God, but the Word of God would enter my heart and spirit from all the above vehicles by any-means-necessary. Since I knew the Word of God for myself, I knew what Word to keep in my heart and spit out what did not coincide with my personal biblical beliefs. Yes, I continued to attend my home church with my family and husband every Sunday during this time, except when I ministered in other churches as a choir director.

At our home church, some congregants knew my husband was going to eventually leave and divorce me. In fact, two years before leaving our home, he communicated to some of the pastors and leadership of the church his intentions to divorce me. As the reader, I know you are probably formulating a quick opinion. Some family and friends thought I should tell my husband if he wanted to leave, leave now. Why wait? Others felt that I should leave my home church, too. I didn't leave our family church or ask him to leave the home during this time because I didn't feel the leading of the Lord to do so, thinking that maybe my husband would reconsider and stay in the marriage. However, when my husband left our home on February 1st, I officially removed my membership from that church roll the very next Sunday!

It was during this time (1999) that my daughter Joy and I started attending my current church, which had a membership of 1,900 people. My new church was so very different from my former 150-member church. At this new church, no one knew of my story and pain. I could attend worship services, hide out in the pew every Sunday, hear the Word of God, and return home blessed! My pastor knew there were people like me hiding out in the congregation, but didn't know who we were. He did his best to minister to each of us. The hurt of abandonment from my husband and former home church hindered me from joining this church for two long years.

Through my pain, I was constantly waiting to hear from the Lord whether I should join this church. Joy, my fifteen-year-old daughter, immediately felt led by God to join the church, doing so during one cold snowy Tuesday night during Bible study. Joy came home excited that she had aligned her church membership with her new church. Since she was a minor, I told her I made decisions for our family. Joy said, "The Lord told me to go forward to the altar and join the church." Oh well, I guess I wasn't the only one listening to God's small, still voice.

My thirteen-year-old son, Mark, also felt an immediate and strong pull to join my parent's church. My hurt and pain may have hindered me from hearing the Lord about where to place my church membership. I am so blessed that my children wanted to continue attending church, and the one of their choosing. Both children became involved in several ministries in their respective churches. During this time, I was attending three morning services mostly each Sunday. My son Mark's church service was at 8:00 AM; Joy's service church was at 9:00 AM; my service, where I was the choir director, was at 11:00 AM. Thank God that each of the three churches was within a half hour of each other. Yes, three worship services a Sunday! One Sunday morning, I had three communions. After two years of dating my new church, I went forward to the altar during the call to discipleship for church membership, and I am now where I belong!

Since 1997, the Lord has literally given me specific words

from heaven each month. These words, which I wrote down, I called "Jesus' Vocabulary Words." Some words have been victory, peace, and praise. Jesus would confirm these words in scripture, sermons, and conversations with other believers in Christ.

Many people daily wait to hear a word or words from the Lord. A minister stated in a revival one day that he was so desperate for a word from the Lord that he would not have cared if a stranger in the street were giving it to him.

In the late 90s, as I drove to work every weekday, Gospel Highway 11, Philadelphia's first all-Gospel radio station, played a song every day at 8:00 AM entitled "We Need a Word From the Lord" by Thomas Whitfield. Oh, how this song ministered to me as I drove to work each day. Although Thomas Whitfield has passed away, his music and words remain with us.

God will have the last word, and it will be good! Walk and live the Word of God.

Discussion Questions

1. Is there a favorite verse or a passage of scripture that has helped you during a difficult time in your life? Explain how.
2. Consider sharing your favorite verse or passage of scripture with someone who needs encouragement through a text message, email, card, voicemail, or in person. Who would benefit from you sharing your favorite verse or passage of scripture?
3. Has there been a time in your life when you felt God was silent? You were waiting for "a Word" from the Lord, direction, or guidance, and heard nothing from Him? How did you handle that situation?
4. If that situation ever happens again, how will you handle it in the future? What scripture(s) will you use to help you while waiting for guidance and direction from the Lord?

Lesson Learned – **"Walking and Living The Word"**

My Prayer From The Word of God

Psalm 27:4-5, 7-14 (KJV)

4 One thing have I desired of the Lord, that will I seek after; that I may dwell in the house of the Lord all the days of my life, to behold the beauty of the Lord, and to enquire in his temple.
5 For in the time of trouble he shall hide me in his pavilion: in the secret of his tabernacle shall he hide me; he shall set me up upon a rock.
7 Hear, O Lord, when I cry with my voice: have mercy also upon me, and answer me.
8 When thou saidst, Seek ye my face; my heart said unto thee, Thy face, Lord, will I seek.
9 Hide not thy face far from me; put not thy servant away in anger: thou hast been my help; leave me not, neither forsake me, O God of my salvation.
10 When my father and my mother forsake me, then the Lord will take me up.
11 Teach me thy way, O Lord, and lead me in a plain path, because of mine enemies.
12 Deliver me not over unto the will of mine enemies: for false witnesses are risen up against me, and such as breathe out cruelty.
13 I had fainted, unless I had believed to see the goodness of the Lord in the land of the living.
14 Wait on the Lord: be of good courage, and he shall strengthen thine heart: wait, I say, on the Lord.

CHAPTER 6

IT'S IN THE PEN

I learned that I could still write songs of praise, worship, and honor to God while in the valley. A composer draws inspiration from the depths of their heart. Many composers and singers often say their work reflects the experiences in their lives. If I were to produce my debut project, it would be titled, *Songs From My Heart*, and it would feature the following original compositions:

Songs From My Heart

1. "Let the Lord Lead You"
2. "Shine"
3. "As For Me and My House, We Will Serve the Lord"
4. "A Vessel of Honor"
5. "When We Go to Battle"
6. "Perfect Peace"
7. "We Give Thanks to Thee, O God"
8. "Just For You and Me"
9. "Song of Jude"

During the time of my separation and divorce proceedings, I composed songs 5, 6, 7, and 8. Where did I get the time, energy, and inspiration to compose the above songs? The melodies and thoughts of my heart came through my fingers and mouth as I read God's Word and walked in the valley. The above fictitious name of my project, *Songs From My Heart*, may not have been number one on the Billboard Gospel Charts, but the message of the songs that God inspired me to write has spoken to the hearts of the people to whom I have ministered and to the members of the churches and choirs with whom I have worked in Pennsylvania, New Jersey, New York, Delaware, and St. Vincent and the Grenadines. More importantly, my own songs have touched me where I had a hole longing for it to be filled by God. God gave me a song!

If I were producing my first project with music from other composers as well, I would add the following songs:

Songs To My Heart by Others

1. "Great is Thy Faithfulness" (T. Chisholm/ W. Runyan)
2. "I Need Thee Every Hour" (Annie S. Hawks)
3. "Through It All" (Andre Crouch)
4. "Stand Still" (Carol Antrom)
5. "My Soul Loves Jesus" (Charles H. Mason)
6. Sunday School Medley: "The Lord is My Shepherd,", "Cares Chorus," (Kelly Willard), and "He's Able" (Paul E. Paino)
7. "Order My Steps" (Glenn Burleigh)
8. "My Tribute" (To God Be The Glory) (Andre Crouch)
9. "Sovereign" (Carol Antrom)
10. "It Is Well With My Soul" (H. Spafford/Phillip Bliss)

JOURNALING – Write it Down

As I composed songs, I also used my pen in another manner – I started journaling my thoughts and emotions. Although I was a schoolteacher for thirty-four years and essay writing was one skill I taught, I didn't begin my personal journaling until I walked into my extreme valley experience. After all, "What's good for the goose is good for the gander." I gave my students writing prompts to aid them with a focus for their daily journals. But in my instance, my daily valley life experiences brought forth many writing prompts for me.

Throughout the months, years, and up to the present, God's goodness and faithfulness are displayed in written form throughout my journal entries. Writing in my personal journals gave me a vehicle for the expression of my feelings, thoughts, and reflections. The journals also gave me an opportunity to note the encouraging words I have heard and received from family, friends, ministers, televangelists, personal devotions, and God. I also noted my goals for the year and future in my journals. Some goals were met, while others were not. However, setting goals aids one in striving for progress and growth.

During this time, my life circumstances were unsettling, but writing my personal thoughts, feelings, and goals was therapeutic and healing for my soul. When I periodically reread my journals, I reflect on the goodness of the Lord. The journals show how the Lord has healed my hurts, satisfied my longings, helped me achieve many of my goals, and assisted me with paying my children's college bills. Throughout the years, when I think about throwing a pity party, I reread portions of my journals to remind me of God's faithfulness and goodness! Instead of a pity party, I must give God praise!

During personal devotions, and while I was meditating on God's Word, God also gave me messages for the body of Christ and for myself. I have delivered only a few of them to women's groups. In the past, the Lord gave me words for songs, but now He has included sermon notes, too.

My journal writings allowed me to vent my feelings and emotional upheavals. I see my growth, achievements, and God's faithfulness vividly as I occasionally review my writings. It is a testament to God's interventions in my life that I have come out to a wealthy place (Psalm 66:12). My journals are for God and me alone. Journaling is my personal testament to God's help in my life. Nonetheless, there are a few entries I would like to share.

- July 8, 1998 PM

LAVERNE [MY SISTER] said to me, God is not pleased with what the legs of man can do. The wrath of man does not accomplish the purposes of God (James 1:20).

- July 9, 1998

2 CHRONICLES 34:26-27 "Because your heart is tender, and you humbled yourself before God when you heard His words against this place."

- December 29, 1999

Jesus knows all about Marlene.
- my failures
- my shortcomings
- my heartache

And He still chooses to love me. He restores my life (soul) and brings hope to every area of my life.

WHILE IN THE VALLEY

- February 19, 2000

I cannot believe a year ago I lost my pocketbook at the PFT Conference. The Lord blessed. It was found and turned over to me.

1999 Victories

1. Roof leak fixed – February
2. My lost pocketbook was returned during a teacher's conference - February 18
3. New front steps and pathway – August
4. New back steps - kitchen entrance - October
5. New car – November (Car accident in June 1999)

- March 15, 2000

In the middle of my STORM, I can enjoy life. God has my breakthrough already planned.

Journaling is a helpful tool for anyone who is in crisis and wants to write about his or her feelings and thoughts. This free therapeutic tool is a great way to express feelings, whether good, bad, or indifferent. A journal is also a record of one's life events and a vehicle to reminisce about the past at a future time. While my journals are in written format, many others prefer electronic formats and utilize applications on devices like computers, iPads, smartphones, and even blogs. My journals are a written reminder of what God has done for my family and me. Even now, when I contemplate entering into a personal pity party, I gather one or more of my journals, hold them in my hand, and read about what God has done for me in the past (I have a glorious history with God). I then give God praise for all that He has done in my life.

In my March 6, 2000 journal entry, I created a K-W-L (What I <u>Know</u>, What I <u>Want</u> to Know, What I <u>Learned</u>) chart – Who God Is, Myself, Family, and Friends – based on Second Corinthians 1:8-11. A K-W-L, which is a graphic organizer, is a visual tool to assist students with organization on a topic. My K-W-L chart wasn't filled in, but I understood what I was saying to myself. If God chooses never to do another thing for me, I praise Him for all that He has done for me. I am ever so grateful. "It's in the Pen" is a lesson I continue to use in my life.

Discussion Questions

1. Have you ever written a poem, a mantra, or lyrics to a song to assist you in your walk in the valley or at the end of the trial? Please share it.
2. Write or compose a short four-line poem on joy, trials, or brokenness.
3. Write a poem based on a scripture that helps you walk through your trials.
4. Is there a song(s) that you sang to lift your spirits and soul? Name the song(s). How did the song(s) lift your spirits?
5. Have you gone back at a later time and re-read your journal writings? What were your thoughts about your past writings?
6. Some people share their past and/or present journals with others. Would you consider sharing your journal entries?

Lesson Learned – **"It's in the Pen"**

CHAPTER 7

GIVE GOD GLORY

"Oh that men would praise the Lord for His goodness, and for
His wonderful works to the children of men!"
Psalm 107:31

*L*ift your hands and give God praise. For many, this is very difficult to remember when going through difficult, tiresome, and arduous trials. It is ten times easier to complain and enter into a personal one-person pity party than to give God praise. The devil wants to steal our praise. Don't let him have it! John 10:10 reminds us that "The thief cometh not, but for to steal, and to kill, and to destroy: I am come that they might have life, and that they might have it more abundantly."

Don't let the devil steal your praise and joy. God wants us to praise our way out of our difficulties, even when everything looks bleak. Life is about choices. The decision is yours. Choose to be a praiser.

I had to make a conscious decision to give God praise. There are so many reasons to give God praise. Your husband left you; praise God for God's strength to endure the situation. Praise God for a great measure of health. Praise God because He is omnipotent. Praise Him because you have the means to support your children and yourself. Praise God that you have a house to live in. I can go on and on and on. "Oh that men would praise the Lord for His goodness, and for his wonderful works to the children of men!" (Psalm 107:8). For me, there was victory in the praise.

Did God wake you up this morning, clothed in your right mind? Is there food on your table? Are you healthy? Don't squawk! Give glory to God, saints. Let all the people praise Him!

During this most difficult time in my life, I learned to praise God although I didn't feel like it or want to. In 1906, Leila Naylor wrote a song entitled "Let All the People Praise Him." This song speaks of praising the Lord. The chorus states: "Let all the people praise Him! Let all the people praise Him! Let all the people praise Him! Let all the people praise Him forever and forever more." God is so worthy of our praises.

Please don't get the wrong impression that I had praise on my lips twenty-four hours a day. There were many times I wanted to enter into a pity party. My litany was, "Lord, I was a good girl. How is this happening to me?" Wait a minute! Just because I tithed, consistently attended worship services, and had personal daily devotions did not give me an exemption card from troubles and tribulations. I knew this in theory, but my heart and lips kept repeating the litany.

During the separation, I sometimes felt I had a right to bemoan, cry, and have people feel sorry for me. No, I do not have that right! Get up and give God the glory and the praise! The devil hates to hear people give God praise. Praise sends the devil on his way. Praises to God are like curse words to Satan. Praising the Lord helped me walk in the valley.

God knows what you are going through, and He is here to help you. Does God want to hear your complaints? Yes, He is very concerned about your pain, but He wants to hear praise come from your lips. We were placed on this earth to give Him glory, even while going through tough times. This concept was hard for me, but I learned to give Him praise!

Remember, we aren't the only ones who are going through, went through, or will go through tough times. Do you remember Job and Joseph in the Old Testament, and Steven, Mary, and Paul in the New Testament? Praise God that they blessed God and didn't curse God and die. Paul and Silas were on lockdown in jail, but sang hymns and songs, and people were saved! Acts 16:25 states, "And at midnight Paul and Silas prayed, and sang praises unto God: and the prisoners heard them."

From Biblical times to the present day, there are people who are facing life issues ten times worse than what you or I are going through. Should we give them a name? You know who they are. I am speaking of the people who have suffered tragedies, extreme financial hardships, foreclosures, debilitating health issues, and unemployment.

God deserves and desires all the glory. He is worthy to be praised for just who He is. Sometimes if you take a praise break or a Give-God-Glory break, you will feel better. The focus is not on you, but on God. As a little girl, I can remember the older church ladies giving God the praise and glory for everything. It was a blessing to see them excited about Jesus although they had issues and pain in their bodies.

I visually remember one of the oldest women at church who had arthritis throughout her entire body, jumping high into the air while praising God. Where had her pain gone? She wanted to praise the Lord and nothing stopped her. The older persons in the congregation loved to leap for joy and praise their God. It was a blessing to see them excited about Jesus although they had issues and pain in their bodies. I cannot testify to having the same glee as they had, but I've learned to give God a shout of praise and sometimes a joyful dance in His presence.

My former teen Bible teacher from a Christian summer camp in the Poconos encouraged me during my valley experience with Isaiah 61:3. It says God gives us "the garment of praise for the spirit of heaviness." I read it, spoke it, and relied on it to get me through my life-changing events. You don't always need a pill, a self-help book, a new dress or suit, retail therapy, or another relationship to get through your problems or a divorce. First, give God praise! I didn't do it at first, but I now know that is what I should have done. Now I incorporate Isaiah 61:3 into my life. I put on a garment of praise for the spirit of sadness or despondency. I had to because I wanted my burdens lifted.

Praise lifts the weight of sadness. No matter what we are going through, God deserves all the praise. Praising God takes the focus off of me and onto God. I have learned and relied on this lesson over and over! I lift my hands and voice to the Lord wherever I am. I praise God in the shower, while driving, cooking, in personal devotional time, in church, while singing, and while playing the piano. There is nothing like going into a dance or a shout while getting dressed. Take a praise break all by yourself! There is no reason to walk around sad and despondent. God has it all under control. Trust and never doubt Him! He will bring you out of your troubles. The Bible states, "Let everything that hath breath praise the Lord." Psalm 150:6a. I have lots of breath and praise for the Lord! Praise the Lord! Praise ye the Lord! I will sing of His mercy! God has never failed me! I have history with God!

Just because we are going through something does not mean everything in our lives shuts down. We are still to give God the glory and praise for everything that happens in our lives. I have heard many pastors and ministers state that some people lost their minds while going through a divorce. Thank God I was able to keep my mind intact. (Some people would not agree.)

God deserves and desires all the glory. He is worthy to be praised just for who He is. Sometimes if you take a praise break or a take a Give-God-Glory break, you will feel better. The focus is not on you, but on God.

It is ironic that while I was married, my spouse gave me a scripture verse that has become one of my favorite Bible verses, "Thou wilt shew me the path of life: in thy presence is fullness of joy, at thy right hand there are pleasures for evermore" (Psalm 16:11). I praise God that I know that my joy comes from The Lord.

God's Glory or My Glory

Although I loved to give God glory and praise, I noticed that there was something disturbing in my walk with God. God showed and taught me something about myself that I didn't know or like about myself. God showed me something so deep that I could not believe it. Then He showered me with multiple examples so I would not get it confused or have a misunderstanding.

There were times when I wanted the glory that was due to Jesus. The lights needed to be on me and not on the Jesus in me. Shine the light on me! I am not really sure how this happened. I, like Samson in the Bible, knew where my strength came from. Let us be very clear; I know that all that I am and have is because of Jesus. Why I wanted God's glory was part of my fleshly desires.

My next course of action through the learning of this lesson was to continually give all glory to God and not have the light shine on me. Galatians 5:24 says, "And they that are Christ's have crucified the flesh with the affections and lusts."

It is by God's grace that I can sing solos, perform, sing in choral groups, and teach vocal parts to choirs. I have overused my voice during the thirty-four years of teaching through yelling, forced singing, and speaking loudly while teaching. But God allowed me to keep some of my upper vocal range and not experience vocal pain. (I have had vocal pain in the past.) I cannot believe I would sometimes steal God's glory when I sang. Romans 8:13 states, "For if ye live after the flesh, ye shall die: but if ye through the Spirit do mortify the deeds of the body, ye shall live." I must die daily to the lusts of the flesh and yield to the Spirit of God. Accolades, my resume, and compliments sometimes make my head swell. One particular time, I asked not to be introduced with my resume. I wanted to speak through the power of the Holy Spirit and not in the flesh. There are a million more stellar resumes than mine, but hearing my accomplishments created a swelled head.

During this time, Jesus showed me myself in no uncertain terms. I constantly had to go before the Lord and ask for forgiveness and help! The process took time, and the Lord has to continually deal with me. It is all about Jesus. No flesh should glory (First Corinthians 1:31). "He deserves all the glory and the praise." (This is a line from the song I composed entitled "Let Your Light So Shine.") First Chronicles 17:20 says, "O Lord, there is none like thee, neither is there any God beside thee, according to all that we have heard with our ears." There is none like him. I am not sure if the Apostle Paul or the Corinthians had a problem like mine, but the Apostle Paul helps me understand where the glory belongs. There are enough scriptures to keep me in line, but I must yield to do what the Bible says. Help me, Lord!

> "That no flesh should glory in his presence.
> That, according as it is written, He that glorieth,
> let him glory in the Lord."
> (First Corinthians 1:29 & 31)

Each one of my choirs sings Clint Brown's song "Give God the Glory. Give Him the Praise." We use it as a processional, choral piece, and/or an offering selection. This song selection is appropriate for nearly any part of the worship service. The words of the song serve as a powerful reminder to offer glory to God.

Get into His presence! Thank Him for who He is! Thank Him for the lessons learned, the battles lost, and the victories won. Give God glory! Hallelujah! Give God praise! Hallelujah!

Discussion Questions

1. Why is it difficult for some people to give God glory and praise when going through difficult times?
2. How do you give God praise when going through a fiery trial or valley experience?
3. What feelings or emotions have you felt when you gave God the glory in your valley experience?
4. When was the last time you had to give God the glory and the praise, although the situation wasn't pleasant?
5. Has there been a time in your life when you were on the right track by giving God the glory and then the focus shifted onto you and not on God? Did you immediately realize the shift? What did you do? (That is, what did you change, confess, and/or apologize to the Lord.)
6. Why do some people want so much attention focused on them?

Lesson Learned – "Give God Glory"

CHAPTER 8

FASTING, SINGING, AND PRAYER

During my Christian walk, for important decisions in my life, I have occasionally fasted. In the year 2001, one Sunday morning during church, I was given a flyer from the Christian education department about the upcoming classes for the spring semester. One of the course offerings was a class on fasting. Here it is! I figured I now had time to go deeper with God since I needed additional help while in my valley experience. I registered for the class and it revolutionized my life. We learned about the different types of fasts, the reasons for fasting, how to fast, and how to exercise and take care of the bodies that God had given us.

Fasting

During an informal conference with my son's high school principal, I was reminded of this very fact. My son's Spanish grade on his report card was the topic in question. As we talked, I spoke about my concern for my son to do better in his classes. She stated, "Mrs. Cooper, some things only come by fasting and prayer." I cannot describe the shock that I felt when I heard those words from her! Where am I? Did I just get a word from the Lord, from an inner city Philadelphia public high school principal? Yes, I did! And I received it, too! (Both of our pastors are friends, and our churches have worshipped together in the past.)

Among my favorite hobbies are playing tennis, traveling, food and clothes shopping, cooking, and reading. But during this season in my life, I had to learn how to temporarily abstain from food for one meal on a weekly basis. This was a challenging endeavor, but I managed to achieve it. Earlier, I talked about tapping into God's power source through prayer. God's Word also states that some things only come by fasting and prayer (Matthew 17:21).

Prayer

While growing up in a Christian home, I watched and experienced my parents' daily prayer life. Daily they prayed together, and we had family devotions every night unless we were in church that evening for a service or ministry. The greatest legacy my parents left for my four siblings and I was learning to stay on our knees before the Lord and have a viable prayer life.

When I first heard the words "I want a divorce" from my husband, my life and emotions went into a tailspin. At 1:00 AM, maybe a week later, I was so distraught that I needed the prayers of my mother. I quietly left my house in my pajamas and went to my parents' house. (My parents and I live on the same street, and I have a key to their home.) My parents were asleep, but I needed my mother! They both awoke when they heard and saw me in their bedroom. I asked if my mother would go with me to another bedroom and pray. My daddy wasn't having that. He said, "Daughter, we will pray right here." Hallelujah for praying parents at any hour of the day or night.

My parents prayed for me and asked God for His help in my life during this time. Although I was thirty-nine years old, I would have loved to have gone to my former bedroom, slept in my childhood bed, and wished all my troubles away. Nonetheless, I returned home with the prayers of her parents.

Prayer and Fasting

I have tried the 40-day fast once or twice, but I usually fast weekly. Fasting is difficult for me. Remember, I love food. Sometimes we have to give up what we want in order to achieve a deeper relationship with Christ. I usually fast one meal a week, but I took a one-year break after my daughter Joy finished medical school. (Joy thought I was still fasting while she was in residency, so I returned to weekly fasting). Although fasting one meal a week does not seem like a tremendous sacrifice, it is a mammoth one for me.

One afternoon, during the school year in 1997, I was fasting during lunchtime. I was interrupted fifty million times by my students trying my classroom doorknob for entrance into my room. So, I decided to go to a quiet place in my classroom where no one could see me from the window of the door. I turned the lights out and locked the door. Nevertheless, my students refused to let me be. Someone must have seen me go into my classroom and not come out during the lunch period. Although the classroom was dark and the door was locked, a couple of students continued to knock until I answered the door. I refused and kept praying. Then they finally left. Little did they know that their teacher was fighting for her life. I was going through a separation, divorce, child support hearings, etc., and they wanted to bother me while I was fasting and praying. Give me a break!

Then my classroom phone rang and rang. I refused to answer. It was lunchtime, and it was my time to eat and pray in peace. The phone stopped ringing. Then the school's secretary made an announcement on the public address system, "Ms. Cooper, please call the office." Now I had to stop praying! I called the office. My students told the office staff that I was in my classroom and I could be dead. The office staff was checking out their suspicions.

There I was, in my classroom, trying to fast and pray because I was in a fight for my life, and my students thought I was dead because I refused to answer the door! Laughing will make the heart glad. God has a sense of humor. Remember, no one knew at school that I was going through a separation or divorce. I didn't have a suicidal demeanor or a hang-my-head-down look. Moreover, I do not even remember what the students wanted. They probably did not want to go outside for recess, and instead, they wanted to hang out in my classroom with all the computers. I did feel blessed that they cared enough to make sure I was all right. I could not blame the devil for trying to keep me from fasting that day. All I wanted to do was fast and pray in peace.

Yes, there have been times when I told the Lord, "This is not a good day for me to fast because I am just too hungry." We have human bodies, and God totally understands. Sometimes fifteen minutes before a fast was over, I had to cut it short and eat a meal. I am still working on my food issues. If you are a psychologist, you may say that I eat to mask the pain of divorce and rejection. You may be right. Food is still an issue with me, and I am dealing with it.

My parents left a legacy of prayer and fasting with us children. My siblings and I could hear our parents praying for each one of us. If there was a problem, my parents would say, "Let's pray about it." Although my earthly father has gone on to heaven, my mother continues to pray with her children and grandchildren about family and personal needs. Communicate with the Father through prayer, fasting, and reading His Word.

The benefits are enormous, and it works! I am a witness! Some things only come through fasting and prayer.

Singing

Singing will make a glad heart. I learned to listen more closely to the words of my favorite hymns while walking through my dark valley experience. I have been listening to and singing hymns my entire life. Hymns, Christian choruses, scripture songs, classical music, and gospel music have been my genres of choice. But in my darkest hour, these songs emanated from the depths of my soul. Many of these songs weren't for anyone's particular listening pleasure but for God alone. The Lord does not care about the quality of your voice. Your voice can sound like a solo operatic singer, a choral singer, a monotone singer, or an off-key singer. Open a church hymnal or find hymns on the Internet or YouTube and sing the old hymns of the faith. Most of the hymn writers had a personal experience that caused them to write their lyrics. Make a joyful noise unto the Lord! Sing some of the songs listed below that have ministered to me, or listen to them and have them minister to your spirit as you listen.

Since my separation, I have sung more hymns in my private time with God, many times with tears streaming down my face. What a blessing to remember the hymns and have these songs in my life! Believe it or not, I wasn't singing fictitious songs like "He Done Me Wrong," or "Oh No He Didn't." I had to sing songs that would uplift my spirit and bring me solace, comfort, and joy! The singing of hymns should be one backbone of the church! Congregational hymns have themes dealing with prayers, praise, adoration, and worship. Besides teaching me Bible verses when I was a child, I am thankful to all my former pastors, choir directors, Sunday school teachers, camp counselors, Vacation Bible School teachers, and my mother for teaching me hymns, choruses, and scriptural songs. My mother, my first piano teacher, also used hymns unfamiliar to me in my piano lessons for sight-reading exercises to build my piano skills.

There is a new movement in some Christian churches, wherein the congregation only sings contemporary and praise and worship songs. These congregations miss out on the beautiful old hymn melodies, stories, and powerful messages of faith. My current pastor, Reverend Dr. Alyn E. Waller, unapologetically continues the tradition of singing hymns in our worship services, and for this, I am most happy, especially when accompanied on our church's four manual Rodgers Ruffatti pipe organ. I prefer a hymn accompanied by a grand, lush, majestic setting with an extended modulation leading into the final verse of the hymn. Although I incorporate contemporary and praise and worship songs, spirituals, and gospel into the worship service, I almost never leave out the hymns of the faith.

There are many times I have sung songs to myself when my heart and spirit were greatly despondent. Sometimes, we must encourage ourselves in any way possible. "Grace, Grace, God's Grace," by Daniel B. Towner and Julia H. Johnston was one of the many hymns that ministered to me. This hymn spoke about God's grace that is given to everyone. "Great is thy Faithfulness," "It is Well," and "Blessed Assurance" are three additional beloved hymns of mine. Many of the Christian childhood songs that have ministered to me in my adult life's valley experience include "The Lord is My Shepherd," "Cares Chorus," and "He's Able." How many times have I sung these songs as a child and/or led these songs in the youth groups during camp worship, Vacation Bible School (VBS), and Sunday School every year? Each song comes back to my remembrance. The above songs have lifted my spirits and turned my sadness into joy. Bless the Lord, oh my soul!

Discussion Questions

1. What types of fasts have you been on? (i.e., Daniel Fast, Liquid Fast, one day a week, water-only fast.)
2. How has spiritual fasting been instrumental in your life?
3. If you haven't fasted before, would you consider going on a fast for spiritual insight, growth, direction, or reflection? Why or why not?
4. What are some of your favorite hymns, spirituals, or Christian songs that resonate in your heart?
5. What particular verse or chorus of a hymn, spiritual, or Christian song gives you the most comfort?
6. Is there a childhood song(s) you learned in Sunday School, Vacation Bible School, or overnight or daytime Christian camping, daycare, youth groups or Christian school that comes to your remembrance and holds dear memories? Why that particular song(s)?

LESSON LEARNED – "FASTING, SINGING, AND PRAYER"

CHAPTER 9

JEHOVAH JIREH: GOD PROVIDES

One major lesson that was on my list of lessons learned was that God provides! God has always been a provider in my life, but doubt entered my mind. I had just entered a new phase in my life, and I didn't know if I could succeed by myself. Could I continue to trust God for this phase of my life? I was now a single mom, one wage earner, one driver, etc., but God provided. I was thankful for family and friends who provided me with help when I needed it with my children. Thanks to those people who helped me drive my children to their respective universities for move-in and move-out days. Each of their respective universities was five-to-six hours from our home in the opposite direction from each other. Some of my friends and family members helped me drive to their colleges.

I am grateful for my village of family and friends who supported my children with love, support, financial blessings, and prayer while they were in college and medical school. The village is too numerous to name; your reward is in heaven. God provides.

. . .

Finances

Recently I found past college bills from my children's educational experiences at Harvard and Hampton University. I did not throw away some of those bills because I wanted a reminder of God's provision for my family. I give praise and thanks to God for giving me the finances to send them to the universities of their choice. The money didn't drop out of heaven or fall from trees, but God gave them scholarships, loans, extra jobs from income, money from my paycheck, and favor. Jehovah Jireh is my provider. Although I put some of the tuition payments on my credit cards, I was able to pay them off. (I would advise no one to do this.)

One day I told Joy's financial counselor at Harvard that I had six jobs and wasn't hustling to find another! I needed a little more assistance. Family and friends often informed me that Harvard University had full scholarships for low-income families. However, my teacher's salary was not considered low-income; therefore, I had to work additional jobs to finance her education.

Never was there a time when my children were in danger of being put out of school because of non-payment of tuition. The payments may have been late, but the funds made it to their universities. One time I called the bursar's office at Hampton University and told them that the tuition funds for my son were forthcoming and pleaded for them not to put my son out of his dorm room. The woman in the office started laughing. She said, "Where did you hear those types of stories?" I told her, "I'm just saying…" During the time my children were in college, I continued to tithe from my income to my church, and I still paid those dreaded college bills. What a blessing! God provides!

LAUGHTER

Laughing makes a merry heart. During my valley experience,

WHILE IN THE VALLEY

God allowed me to have many humorous moments. In the book of Psalms, David writes, "A merry heart doeth good like a medicine: but a broken spirit drieth the bones" (Proverbs 17:22). My very first experience concerning this was on the morning after my husband asked me for a divorce. Believe me, I wasn't laughing on that particular morning or even many mornings after that, but the following experience made me laugh and say months later, "Are you serious, Lord?"

On the very next morning, after he asked me for a divorce, I was scheduled to speak on the word "Joy" at a women's prayer breakfast for a church in Philadelphia. Can you believe that in God's infinite wisdom? He laid on the heart of the pastor's wife to invite me to speak on the word "Joy" on January 19, 1997.

God is omnipotent and knows all things. God knew before I was born that my husband would ask for a divorce the night before the women's prayer breakfast. Okay, Lord. Are you serious? With the power of God and a broken heart that was bleeding profusely, I delivered a message on 'Joy.' I clung to Jesus, speaking with His anointing and divine strength. I had nothing to give; Jesus gave the message through me. The women were blessed. During my message, I wasn't ready to share with the women about my earlier night's experience, but I did share about the joy that God gives. Believe it or not, I still have those handwritten message notes from my message on joy. That experience is a testimony to God and His promises. Several years later, I did share with the same women at a prayer breakfast what transpired the night before I spoke to them on the word 'Joy.'

Another humorous moment came when I first called my divorce lawyer for an initial appointment. I told him that my husband didn't want me anymore. The lawyer said, "Don't worry. I want you!" (Cha-Ching! $$) He turned a very sad moment for me into great laughter. My lawyer probably told every woman that line. When one calls a divorce lawyer for the first time, it is not a laughing matter. But with my lawyer's words, I could not stop laughing. One can laugh through one's tears. God has a sense of humor!

Another incident occurred at work. I usually wear business attire to work, and on this particular day I was well-dressed in my Ralph Lauren designer blue suit. When I arrived to school that morning, after observing my attire, my school principal asked if she could have a conversation with me later that day. When our meeting rolled around, she didn't wait for me to come to her office; she came to my classroom to ask me a very important question that was plaguing her. She asked, "Are you going on a job interview today?" (Days earlier, I asked for permission to leave school forty-five minutes early.) I answered, "I am not attending a job interview."

Can I say I was shocked? Initially, I wasn't sure what my principal wanted; I could not bring myself to tell her that I was attending a child support court hearing at Philadelphia's Family Court. Once again, in my sadness, I could only laugh. Did I really look that good?

God often allowed me to laugh out loud (LOL) at certain circumstances during my separation and divorce process. For example, one of my part-time church jobs inquired about my official last name. Wait a minute! The church had used Cooper on my 1099 IRS form for many years. However, this year I filed separately, and the Internal Revenue Service (IRS) informed the church that there was no Marlene Jenkins Cooper. I called the Social Security office in Philadelphia, and they also stated there was no Marlene Jenkins Cooper. In previous years, I jointly filed my income taxes under Marlene Jenkins Cooper with my husband. But why would that make a difference? The Social Security clerk reiterated that there was no Marlene Jenkins Cooper.

When I initially married in 1981, I never took the signed marriage certificate to City Hall. Was I supposed to do that?

Where was the document stating that it was my responsibility to do so? No one told me I was supposed to do that. I was so in love that submitting the signed marriage certificate to City Hall of Philadelphia slipped my mind. Thank God I didn't burn or tear up our marriage certificate while my marriage was disintegrating. Am I really officially married, even though I never took the signed marriage certificate to be entered into the official records at City of Philadelphia?

Having found our marriage certificate, I proceeded to City Hall to have it recorded. After eighteen years of marriage, we were officially registered as Mr. and Mrs. Cooper. Upon the successful completion of the process, The United States Social Security Pennsylvania office updated my maiden name to my now official and legal name, Marlene Jenkins Cooper. However, it's worth noting that this transition occurred just as the divorce paperwork and legal formalities were set to be finalized. Go figure! I learned I could laugh in the midst of this legal craziness, distress, and trouble. Sometimes it was hard to know whether to Laugh out Loud (LOL) or Cry Out Loud (COL)!

Please don't think I laughed out loud throughout my entire divorce process. I was stunned when I was served the petition of divorce papers. When the sheriff, or whoever was sent to serve me the papers, came to my house, he knocked on my front door with a loud bang! Oh my! Who is at my door? I opened the door and was served with the petition of divorce papers. There was no LOL in my spirit on that occasion.

Another possible disastrous experience, which should have made me sad, was laughable too: receiving the official written divorce decree. In May 2003, my divorce attorney informed me that the official decree of divorce and the signing of the document by the judge would not happen until the middle of the summer. When I returned home from my summer cruise at the end of July, there it was in the middle of the mail pile.

The same guest speaker whose husband divorced her also

shared with the class that the official written divorce decree is not what killed the marriage! What a tremendous revelation! Six years later, when I found the official document in my stack of mail, I didn't fall apart, cry uncontrollably, or eat until I could eat no more. What puzzled me was the actual document. It didn't look real. The paper was subpar and the document was of poor photocopying quality. Wait one minute! Is this document real? Am I divorced or legally married? Is someone playing a joke on me?

The next week, I went to the official records office at City Hall. The official clerk stated my document was authentic and official. I purchased another official divorce decree document to be convinced of that fact. What a laughable experience! There are no tears, sadness, or remorse. I am literally laughing because the document does not look authentic. Thanks for the laughs!

I shed many tears while I was in the valley, and the Bible talks about tears. Lord, thank you for teaching me that I could laugh through my pain and have laughter and joy through my tears.

> "Weeping may endure for a night,
> but joy cometh in the morning."
> Psalm 30:5

I WANTED a big celebration for experiencing forty years of life, but it didn't happen. Going through a valley experience of marital discord, separation, and divorce would be my life for the next six years. When I turned fifty, there was a huge celebration. My family and my godmother, Aunt Mildred, gave me a wonderful fiftieth-birthday party at a beautiful venue in Willow Grove, Pennsylvania. The Lord showed me that just because I was forced into divorce proceedings, my life was not over. I could live it up! I learned that I could have positive and enjoyable life experiences while in the valley.

New Passions

My new passion in life has become tennis. Wait a minute! How can a forty-year-old single mother start a new sport? I played junior varsity volleyball in high school, intramural volleyball in college, and was part of an adult Christian bowling league in Philadelphia. After twelve years of taking both children to the tennis center in Philadelphia twice a week for tennis lessons, I decided I should try my hand at it.

Tennis is my new boyfriend. I love it! At forty years of age, I started taking tennis group lessons at an adult evening school on Mondays at 8:00 PM. My friends asked me where I was getting the energy to leave my house at night to start lessons at 8:00 PM. Praise the Lord; I found the energy. There was only one time I fell asleep and missed my tennis class!

Before you ask, I didn't take the yellow tennis ball and pretend the ball was my former husband's head. However, I love hitting the yellow ball with power! The game of tennis has given me a newfound joy. Presently, I have continued my tennis lessons with a private coach, playing in tennis leagues, and enjoying playing with my new friends in the Philadelphia area tennis community. God provides new experiences.

As you may know, God has a sense of humor! God has allowed me to laugh through some of my life experiences, whether good or bad. One day, I was playing singles with one of my friends. While we were playing tennis, her four-year-old grandson, who did not know me, came to the tennis courts with his Pop-Pi to watch our game. The four-year-old boy yelled from the sidelines to me and asked, "Aren't you someone I have seen on television?" I could have kissed that little boy! Thank you, Jesus! Did the little boy think I was Serena Williams or

Venus Williams? Was he implying that I had a body like the Williams sisters, or that I move like lightning as they do, or that I have the spirit to win? Could it be all three? He could not have possibly thought I was Althea Gibson, the first African American who won a Grand Slam in 1956. (My deceased Aunt, Elsie Jordon Bingham played paddleball and tennis with Althea Gibson in the 1940s at the Police Athletic League—PAL—in Harlem, New York, but that was before I was born.) I am not sure what my friend's grandson meant, but he extremely elated me with his comment. From the mouth of babes! Thanks, God, I needed that! God provided laughter during my difficult times.

Recently, swimming has become my rekindled passion. As a child, I loved to swim. Now I swim throughout the entire year at the gym. When I went back to swimming, I took lessons to clear up any bad habits I had acquired over the years. I joined the small group class one week late. On the initial day of my lessons, I was asked to sign a consent form because they were filming my small group. And to my surprise, I discovered that one of the pastors of the church where I serve on the Praise and Worship ministry team was in the same class. Oh no! It was quite amusing to think that I'd be learning swimming skills alongside one of the pastors. I could not stop laughing.

Then, after a series of lessons, my instructor asked me to show the class how to swim properly. Why did he do that? Now I thought I was ready for the Olympics. Several months later, different persons at the gym would ask me, "Is that you swimming in the video on the television screens throughout the gym?" With a broad smile, I said, "Yes!" God provided me with a rekindled love for swimming.

Jehovah Jireh: God Provides. God provided me with money for my children's college bills and household bills, laughter, and new passions for my life. What a blessing! God provides!

Discussion Questions

1. Share two times when God provided in tough times without mentioning money, and how it happened.
2. Name two other names of God and their meanings. How do these relate to you? (i.e., Jehovah Rapha – my healer; when I was healed of recurring stomach pains.
3. Do you have a desire to pursue a passion? If so, what is it, and what's holding you back from exploring it?
4. Have you ever had to abandon a cherished passion due to life circumstances, and do you wish to rekindle the hobby again?
5. What steps are you going to take to pursue a new or forgotten passion?
6. Recollect a time when you perceived God's sense of humor in one of your valley experiences.
7. Reflect on the author's divorce request just before her speaking engagement. Would you have declined to speak to women about joy? What influenced your decision?

LESSON LEARNED – "JEHOVAH JIREH: GOD PROVIDES"

CHAPTER 10

I CAN DO ALL THINGS THROUGH CHRIST

"I can do all things through Christ which strengthens me."
(Philippians 4:13)

Surviving this horrific experience with God's help was not in question. Going through the process of a divorce, which wasn't a piece of cake, was the major problem. Everyone needs strength from a higher power. I am so blessed that I had God to help me through this tiresome journey.

In 1999, during my first year of separation from my husband, I attended a deacon ordination for a dear family friend. The theme for the ordination was "I Can Do All Things Through Christ." At the celebratory meal, each guest had their photograph taken, and each received a church-party favor featuring their picture with the theme inscribed below the picture. The church-party favor continues to be displayed in my bedroom and is a constant reminder that God strengthens me.

The verse "We are more than conquerors" (Romans 8:37) found a permanent place on my refrigerator and serves as a reminder of this principle. (Given my love for food, I encountered this verse frequently.) Since my divorce, I have experienced spiritual growth, continued my walk with God, maintained the family's pre-divorce lifestyle, witnessed both of my children graduate from high school, purchased two new cars, supported both children through their college choices to graduation, completed major repairs and renovations on my home, enjoyed vacations, obtained my Pennsylvania Principal Certification, retired from the School District of Philadelphia, and emerged with my sanity intact, holding my head high.

Although some of the aforementioned achievements are material, the non-tangible are life-sustaining. Have you ever heard a mature Christian saint say, "God is a lifter of my head?" Yes, He is! God will aid us emotionally, physically, financially, and spiritually. My journey wasn't easy or a cakewalk, but God helped me along the way. "You Can Make It," (1993) written by Betty Griffin Keller, is my theme! My mother, Dorothy Jenkins, wrote an additional verse to the song for her church choir.

> If your trials, if your trials seem so hard to bear,
> Don't worry. Don't despair.
> My God answers prayer.
> You can make it.

© 1993 Dorothy Jenkins

You can make it, my friend. Your family, friends, and loved ones may try to assist you in the process, but your ultimate help will come from the Lord. The Lord shows up, and He did in my situation. Although God did not have to, He proved himself to me in so many ways. Maybe your problem is not going through a divorce. Know that the Lord Jehovah is here to help you with any problems you may have. Our Lord God is our Jehovah Jireh, our provider; Jehovah Nissa, the Lord that Heals; El Shaddai, the Lord God Almighty; Jehovah Shalom, The Lord is Peace; Jehovah Tsidkenu, The Lord Our Righteousness; Jehovah Raah,

The Lord is my Shepherd; Jehovah Shammah, The Lord is There; and Jehovah Mekoddishe, The Lord who Sanctifies.

In First Kings 19:7, the prophet Elijah was in distress because Jezebel was after him. God took care of him while he was on his journey in the wilderness. Twice the angel told Elijah, "Arise and eat; because the journey is too great for thee." In Psalm 23, God said he would walk with us, restore our souls, lead us in paths of righteousness, and light our path. God will be the ultimate One who will walk you through your trials and tribulations. He will hold your hand and be your guide and direction. Even when the path is dark, He will lead you. Exercise faith in His promises. God's promises are true and He keeps His promises (Isaiah 26:3&4).

My faith has been stretched and strengthened. The power of God has been revealed in my life through my trials. Communicate with the Father; He is here to help you.

God will not pull and drag you to walk with Him; you must make a conscious decision to choose to walk with Him through your issues of life. My encouragement to you is to rest in Him (Psalm 37:7), cast your cares on Him (First Peter 5:7), trust Him (Proverbs 3:5-6), and let Him Lead you (Psalm 23:4), and all will be well. Notice I didn't say all would be perfect. I found out for myself there is no perfect life.

It has been many years since that frightful night in January 1997. The devil thought he had me. He thought he could take me down. No! No! No! I serve a God who will walk and talk with you. I had to rely on God's love, His Word, and His power to live life day by day, to raise my children, and live victoriously during my separation and divorce. Yes, there were many times when I was sad and despondent; yes, there were times when I felt defeated, but praise the Lord I didn't stay in that place. I give thanks to God for His unmerited favor. Through it all, I thank God for all the trials He brought me through.

While in the valley, I continued to minister to children at

an overnight Christian camp in rural Pennsylvania. I was lying down in my cabin one morning having personal devotions, and God gave me a song that depicted my gratefulness to Him. So I penned the following song and set the words to music:

"We Give Thanks To Thee"

We give thanks to thee, O God
We give thanks to thee, O God
We give thanks to thee, O God
We give thanks for thy name is near.

We give praise to thee, O God
We give praise to thee, O God
We give praise to thee, O God
We give praise for thy works are near.

© 1997 Marlene Jenkins Cooper

I am blessed that both of my children finished high school on time and achieved great things in college. My daughter, Joy, graduated from Harvard University with a Bachelor of Science in African American Studies in June 2006, received a Masters of Science in Public Health from University College London in 2007, became a fellow of the National Institute of Health, researched cervical cancer in Nairobi, Kenya in 2011-2012, obtained a medical degree in May 2013 from Howard University School of Medicine, and is in her fourth year of residency at The Hospital of the University Of Pennsylvania. My son, Mark, graduated from Hampton University in May 2009 with a Bachelor of Science in Marketing and was an assistant manager in a bank until he pursued his own entrepreneurial adventures. At present, I am a retired teacher from the School District of Philadelphia. Praise the Lord! Thanks to everyone who prayed and continues to pray for us!

I am grateful that both of my children continue to have a love for God and regularly attend church. At first, I was quite scared that because of the upheaval in their lives, both of my children might run away from God. One of my dad's best friends stated that my dad and his other best friends had been praying for my children's emotional state and relationship with God. It is not surprising to them that Joy and Mark are still in tune with God.

While I was going through my separation and divorce from my husband, the Lord blessed me with unforeseen blessings:

*In 1999, I was able to keep my mind intact! This is huge!

*In February 2002, I was completely out of debt except for the mortgage on my home.

*I was an invited guest on *Cultural Connection African American School District of Philadelphia*, a television show on how to prepare children for the citywide African American oratorical contest and for entrance into college. I believe they asked me because my daughter, Joy, was the 2002 4th Place African American oratorical contest winner (2002). I also had a winner from my sixth-grade class (2002), and Joy was accepted to Harvard University for enrollment in 2002.

* In 2004, I was chosen to be a member of the first group of fifty-five teachers in the entire state of Pennsylvania who represented the state at a summit/conference in upstate Pennsylvania about our best practices, new ideas, and innovative ways of integrating technology into our respective classrooms to capture the interest of our students. We were called 2004 Pennsylvania Keystone Technology Integrators.

* In 2005, I was awarded "Teacher of the Year" by the Wal-Mart Store in South Philadelphia. This was a great honor.

* To my amazement, a small part of my two-minute submission was chosen to be in a television commercial by Channel 10

NBC's promotion for "Why I Should be Chosen to Co-host 10." (I didn't get the co-host job, but it was fun being on television and watching my submission on television with my middle school students).

* In 2006, the leadership of my current church, Enon Tabernacle Baptist Church in Philadelphia, approached me to take on the role of Vacation Bible School Director.

* With the favor of God on my life, The Lord blessed me to receive four (4) free graduate classes (12 free graduate credits), which aided me in additional educational knowledge for teaching in the classroom, and it helped me attain a higher pay scale.

* In 2013, at fifty-six years of age, I retired after thirty-four years of service to the children of the School District of Philadelphia.

I praise God for all the blessings He has bestowed upon me. The Bible encouraged me by saying, "I can do all things through Christ which strengthens me" (Philippians 4:13). If you use God's strength, you cannot lose. Praise God that I leaned on God for His strength, His power, and His Word.

Going through a divorce and applying for child support through the courts was an arduous task. These two issues were separate law matters. Conferring with a lawyer and going before a judge in my designer Ralph Lauren blue suit was not a great experience either. But, I can do all things through Christ, which strengthens me. (Why do people look their best when in court?)

In the African American gospel musical experience, we often sing about God being a doctor in the sick room and a lawyer in the courtroom. During my child support hearings at Philadelphia District Family Court, I had to go before a judge/magistrate. Until this difficult journey, I had never been before a judge/ magistrate on my behalf. Yes, God is a lawyer in the courtroom. In that courtroom, God proved His Word! The Lord gave me a song in recent years entitled "When We Go to Battle." The chorus is as follows:

> **"When We Go to Battle"**
> When we go to battle, God is on our side.
> God is on our side. God is on our side.
> When we go to battle, God is on our side.
> We can fight; fight and win!
>
> ©2000 Marlene Jenkins Cooper

Another major battle in my life occurred during the festivities of my daughter's eighth-grade graduation (June 1997). Without my permission, discussion, or input, my former husband asked someone to design and sew my daughter's graduation dress. Days prior to the graduation, the dress entered my home. I began to pray and ask the Lord for this dress not to appear at my daughter's eighth-grade graduation. This dress represented disrespect for me (as wife and mother), and was extremely hurtful. I didn't want my daughter wearing a dress that represented such disrespect for me and/or was from someone I didn't approve of. Pictures last a lifetime and I didn't want pictures in the family photo albums of her in that dress. Those pictures would have been lasting memories.

I didn't rant and rage over the idea of the dress to be worn at the graduation, but I let it be known that it was unacceptable and I was in disagreement with the dress. It was a beautiful dress, but it would not hold beautiful memories. This dress would represent another way Satan could create division, discord, and disharmony in our home.

Prayer was my weapon of defense. I prayed and I prayed. I asked the Lord to remove the dress and not to have my daughter wear it at her eighth-grade graduation ceremonies. On the morning of the graduation, I continued to pray. Everyone dressed for the ceremonies. When it was time to leave for the ceremonies, my daughter came down the steps in the outfit she had worn the previous month on Easter Sunday, with no coercion from me. It was a decision she had made on her own. Praise the name of the Lord! This was my prayer. I battle won the battle in the spirit.

Cutting the dress up, hiding the dress, or arguing and fighting over the dress was not in my plan. I agonized in prayer and asked the Lord for His intervention. Joy's ultimate choice was her decision. She was conflicted over the entire dress saga, but in the end, I believe she made the right decision. When we go to battle, we can ask God to go before us and fight for us! We can win!

I don't know what happened to the dress, nor do I care what happened to the dress. The dress disappeared. Praise the name of Jesus. This dress saga may be a small matter to some, but it was major to me. Although Joy had many other graduations years later, for me, her eighth-grade graduation reminds me that God hears our prayers.

Encouragement

Please encourage others as you see them going through difficult times. I believe an easy way of encouraging someone is through a mailed card, email, or text. Since you can't predict the response to in-person encouragement, a mailed card, email, or text provides a convenient way to send your support. You don't have to be there when they receive it. I saved some cards that I received while in the valley, and I reread them occasionally.

The Word of God states in First Thessalonians 5:11 (NIV) "Therefore encourage one another and build up one another, just as in fact you are doing." I thank and praise God for all my family and friends who have said encouraging words to me, sent me a card, or just listened to me whine and/or cry. Thanks.

I also praise God for his teachable lessons and the growth that I have encountered during this time. Tough lessons are an awesome teacher. I just didn't know that the valley experience would last so long! Soon after my trial began, every December 31st at 11:59 PM, I hope to hear the Lord say, "It is over, Marlene. Your trial is now officially over." I guess this was wishful thinking. God does not work on our calendar or timeframe. We cannot determine when our trial and tribulation periods will end. Nonetheless, I am so blessed that I tried to walk in the newness of life each and every day. I didn't always succeed, but it was the desire of my heart to do so. Thank you, Jesus! "For my thoughts are not your thoughts, neither are your ways my ways, saith the Lord" (Isaiah 55:8).

One's life does not stop because a spouse has left the marriage. Know that your heavenly Father will walk with you, talk with you, give you guidance, offer comfort and support, and aid you as you take the difficult journey. My difficult journey was one of going through a divorce. For someone else, it may be losing a job, house, or child. Nevertheless, the above lessons will work in any circumstance that life presents.

My words of encouragement come from the Word of God. Remember, you are more than a conqueror (Romans 8:26). Remember, you are the head, not the tail (Deuteronomy 28:13). Remember, the Lord is your shepherd, and you shall not want (Psalm 23:1). Remember, no weapon formed against you will prosper (Isaiah 54:17). Remember to continue to stand! Finally, remember to quote the scripture, "I can do all things through Christ which strengthens me" (Philippians 4:13). Be encouraged!

I wrote this book because I wanted to share the lessons learned as I walked through the valley and what I learned while experiencing life's challenges. When God speaks, I want to be a superb listener. These lessons learned continually minister to me and I am the better for it. There is growth in my life!

Sharing the lessons learned has been cathartic for me and is a reminder of His goodness to me. I pray you are inspired to victoriously walk through your own valley experience.

While in the valley, I have learned my lessons through the above experiences and the power of the Holy Spirit. School is not over! My experiences have produced growth in my life. My life story is not finished, for God will continue to add more chapters to it. To God be the glory.

"Now unto Him that is able to do exceeding abundantly above all that we ask or think, according to the power that worketh in us, unto him be the glory in the church by Christ Jesus throughout all ages, world without end. Amen."
(Ephesians 3:20 & 21)

Discussion Questions

1. Which individuals in the Bible recognized that they could accomplish all things through Christ who provided them strength?
2. Reflecting on your life, can you recall certain events or challenging moments, where your triumphs and accomplishments were undoubtedly a result of God's intervention?
3. Your story continues to be written. Know that God has your life in His hands. Is this a difficult concept to grasp? Why or why not?
4. What chapter from the book *While In the Valley* had the greatest impact on you?"

LESSON LEARNED - **"I Can Do All Things Through Christ"**

ABOUT THE AUTHOR

Marlene Jenkins Cooper is the author of four books, *While in the Valley: Walking With God Through Divorce, Grace Notes: Five-Minute Inspirational Devotionals for the Church Choir, Musicians, and Friends of Music, Life 101: Money Management and Adulting Made Simple,* which won a 2021 Finalist award from American Writing Awards, and her latest release, *It's Not Worth The Weight: A 90-Day Weight Loss Devotional.*

Marlene Jenkins Cooper is an actively engaged member of Enon Tabernacle Baptist Church. She takes part in various ministries, including music, youth scholarship, counseling, and serving as a devotionalist on the prayer line ministry. As the host of the podcast *Grace Notes: Devotion at the Piano with Marlene,* she shares her spiritual insights based on scripture with sacred music.

Having retired from the School District of Philadelphia, Marlene holds an illustrious career spanning thirty-four years. She began as a general vocal music teacher and later embraced the role of a computer specialist/teacher. She has received recognition from various organizations for her passionate teaching style and commitment to education.

Ms. Cooper holds music education degrees from Temple University and The King's College. Additionally, she pursued further graduate studies in computer technology at Temple University. She is the parent of two adult children and a loving grandmother to one granddaughter.

Besides writing, Ms. Cooper enjoys a diverse range of activities, including reading, traveling, cooking, swimming, and playing tennis. Marlene Cooper's greatest desire is to lead more people into the Kingdom of God and encourage people to live victorious Christian lives.

Website – marlenejenkinscooper.com
    Email – marlenjenkinscooper@gmail.com
    Facebook
    https://www.facebook.com/AuthorMarleneJenkinsCooper/

FEEDBACK AND SUPPORT

I appreciate your purchase and taking the time to read my book. Your support means a lot to me, and I genuinely hope you found the book valuable. If you enjoyed it, I kindly request you to consider sharing it with your loved ones and leaving an online review on Amazon, Goodreads, and/or your favorite book website. Your feedback and support are invaluable to me, as they enable me to pursue my passion. If you'd like to leave a review, please visit *While in the Valley* on Amazon and Goodreads. Thank you once again!

Steps to Leaving a Review on Amazon
    1. Go to Amazon.com and log into your account.
    2. Look for the book *While in the Valley* at https://www.amazon.com/stores/Marlene-Jenkins-Cooper/author/B08KS5YGPV
    3. Click on the book's title and go to its product page.
    4. Scroll down to the "Customer Review" section of the page.
    5. Give a rating (out of 5 stars) and/or write a review in the text box provided.
    Thank you very much.

ALSO BY

MARLENE JENKINS COOPER

Books and eBooks

While in the Valley: Walking With God Through Divorce

Grace Notes: Five-Minute Inspirational Devotionals for the Church Choir, Musicians, and Friends of Music

Life 101: Money Management and Adulting Made Simple

It's Not Worth The Weight: A 90-Day Weight Loss Devotional

QR code for all Marlene Jenkins Cooper books

Podcast

Grace Notes: Devotions at the Piano with Marlene

https://grace-notes.captivate.fm

https://podcasts.apple.com/us/podcast/grace-notes/id1567256758

https://podcasts.google.com/feed/
aHR0cHM6Ly9mZWVkcy5jYXB0aXZhdGUuZm0v
Z3JhY2Utbm90ZXM

www.ingramcontent.com/pod-product-compliance
Lightning Source LLC
Chambersburg PA
CBHW050436010526
44118CB00013B/1551